THE
COMPASSIONATE,
BUT
PUNISHING GOD

THE
COMPASSIONATE,
BUT
PUNISHING GOD

A Canonical Analysis of Exodus 34:6–7

NATHAN C. LANE

PICKWICK *Publications* · Eugene, Oregon

THE COMPASSIONATE, BUT PUNISHING GOD
A Canonical Analysis of Exodus 34:6–7

Pickwick Publications
An Imprint of Wipf and Stock Publishers
199 W. 8th Ave., Suite 3
Eugene, OR 97401

www.wipfandstock.com

ISBN 13: 978-1-60608-792-3

Cataloging-in-Publication data:

Lane, Nathan C.

The compassionate, but punishing God : a canonical analysis of Exodus 34:6–7 / Nathan C. Lane.

x + 166 p. ; 23 cm. Includes bibliographical references and index.

ISBN 13: 978-1-60608-792-3

1. Bible. O.T. Exodus XXXIV, 6–7—Criticism, interpretation, etc. 2 1. Bible. O.T. Exodus—Criticism, interpretation, etc. 3. Bible. O.T.—Canonical criticism. I. Title.

BS1245.2 L38 2010

Manufactured in the U.S.A.

To Trey and Kolton—
my mountains of boundless energy

Contents

Acknowledgments

It is impossible to express adequate thanks to all who have contributed to this long journey. I am especially grateful to Dr. W. H. Bellinger Jr. who has provided significant help along the way by means of encouragement, corrections and advice. This work is markedly better because of his service as my mentor. I would also like to thank Dr. Joel S. Burnett and Dr. Kimberly Kellison for their keen editorial remarks and guidance along the way. A special thank you goes to all of my colleagues at Baylor and Palm Beach Atlantic who have made this journey a happy one. The largest praise, however, goes to my wife, Kristi, who has sacrificed in countless ways during our marriage so that I can do this "work." Without her words of encouragement and help in bearing the burden, I could never have finished.

1

Introductory Matters

INTRODUCTION

The text of Exod 34:6–7 stands as one of the most evocative of the entire Old Testament. The words and images of this text have inspired numerous parallels[1] and countless echoes in the texts of ancient Israel. In fact, parallels exist in all three of the major divisions of the Old Testament. These parallels show that it was one of the most generative texts for the ancient community. Its influence has also extended into medieval and modern Jewish hermeneutics as the texts outline what has become called the "Thirteen Attributes of God." These attributes bear both literary and liturgical importance as they are often recited aloud in the synagogue on festival days and other holy days as the Ark is opened and the Torah scroll is removed.[2]

The evocative nature of the text arises from its rich, but diverse imagery and its place in the narrative of Exodus. The text comes in a theophany situated at the climax of the narrative of Exodus 32–34. These chapters deal with the golden calf rebellion and YHWH's subsequent forgiveness of the people and renewal of the covenant. In Exodus 32, the people turn to the Golden Calf after Moses' time on Sinai has been unduly delayed. When he descends the mountain at YHWH's urging,

---

1. Exod 20:5c–7; 33:19; Num 14:18; Deut 5:9–11; 7:9; 2 Kgs 13:23; 2 Chr 30:9; Neh 9:17; 9:31; Pss 25:6; 78:38; 86:5, 15; 99:8; 103:8; 106:45; 111:4; 112:4; 116:5; 145:8; Jer 30:11; 32:18; Dan 9:9; Joel 2:13; Jon 4:2; Nah 1:3; Mic 7:18–20. Parallels also occur in the Apocrypha (Sir 2:11; 2 Esd 7:132–40), Qumran literature (Damascus Document 2:2–13), and the New Testament (Luke 1:50,58,72,78; 10:37; Rom 9:15–16).

2. Sarna, *Exodus = [Shemot]*, 216.

he finds their sin. YHWH initially intends to destroy the Israelites, but Moses intercedes on the people's behalf and diverts YHWH's anger. After Moses enters the camp, he instructs the Levites to punish those who had worshipped the calf. In Exodus 33, Moses returns to the mountain to again receive the tablets of the covenant. While there, he again intercedes for the Israelites to ensure YHWH presence with them as they go into the land. Moses also requests to see God's glory. YHWH agrees, but only partially—allowing Moses to see the deity's back area. In Exodus 34, new tablets are made and Moses is granted his theophany. In the theophany, YHWH gives Moses this self-proclamation in 34:6–7:[3] "YHWH, YHWH, The gracious and compassionate God, slow to anger and great in loving kindness and truth, maintaining loving kindness to thousands, and taking away iniquity, transgression and sin. However, he will surely not acquit the guilty, visiting the iniquity of the parents on the children and their children unto the third and fourth generation." After this revelation, the deity renews the covenant and gives further covenant stipulations. The pericope of 32–34 ends with Moses' face shining radiantly as he descends the mountain and reports the happenings to the people.

The bipolar nature of the imagery of the credo also contributed to its evocative nature. The first "compassionate pole" rehearses attributes of YHWH that emphasize his positive characteristics. The nation found solace in the loving, slow to anger and compassionate God who was always ready to forgive them for their transgressions. The attributes associated with this compassionate God formed the major pool from which the ancient Israelites drew to express their faith. For example in Num 14:18, Moses reminds God of these compassionate characteristics in order to persuade the deity to forgive the Israelites. The psalmist in Psalm 86 confesses YHWH's positive characteristics as part of the psalmist's acknowledgement that God is different from those trying to kill him (86:15). Jonah even laments these positive characteristics because YHWH did not destroy the Ninevites (Jonah 4:2). These positive characteristics were primary in the theology of ancient Israel.

The second "judgmental pole" also provided a stock of images for the nation. The nation did not shun or edit away these alternative portrayals of their deity. Instead, they kept the images and used them at differing

---

3. There is some disagreement about who actually speaks these words, Moses or YHWH. This problem will be addressed in chapter 2.

times to taunt their neighbors and often even to chastise themselves. For example, Exod 20:4 emphasizes the judgment pole to remind the ancient Israelites not to worship any idols of YHWH. Nahum uses the attributes to taunt the Ninevites that their soon coming destruction would be fierce (1:3). These harsh judgmental images also provided a core aspect of Israel's description of YHWH.

HISTORY OF RESEARCH

The text of Exod 34:6–7 has received a substantial amount of scholarly attention. Historically, the credo of Exodus 34 has been approached diachronically and synchronically—with the former bearing most of the interpretive weight. Very little attention has been given to the place of the text and its parallels in the final form of the canon. The following section will outline the two different styles of historical analyses of the text. Only the major works addressing the text will be examined.

Diachronic Approaches

In 1957, Josef Scharbert published the most thorough form-critical article on the credo.[4] Scharbert's article begins by dividing Exod 34:6–7 into nine different sections with some sections having multiple components.[5] It then examines several of the parallels to see which components are the most pervasive and which are typically censured. He argued that the Deuteronomist modified the tradition of the Jahwist and the Elohist. The Deuteronomist used the texts to show that grace always comes from an alliance with YHWH and his promise and to show that YHWH naturally maintains an alliance with Israel.[6]

Scharbert finds a postexilic *Sitz im Leben* for the final form of the credo. His argument rests on two pillars. First, he argues that the later parallels of the credo rely more heavily on the first, compassionate pole.[7] Later rehearsals are almost exclusively dependent on YHWH's mercy. The portion of the credo that emphasizes judgment "to the third and fourth

4. Scharbert, "Formgeschichte und Exegese von Ex 34,6f und Seiner Parallelen," 130–50.

5. Ibid., 132.

6. Ibid., 136.

7. Ibid., 149.

generation" is never rehearsed. Second, a reversal of generational curses occurs in the postexilic theology of Jeremiah and Ezekiel.[8] In Jeremiah 31 and Ezekiel 18, the prophets overturn the older tradition of children paying for the sins of their parents. For Scharbert, this shows that the credo exhibited some theological development during the exile and after. As the nation experienced the harsh realities of the exile, it emphasized the mercy and grace of YHWH over against the punishing aspect of the second pole.

In 1959, Thorir Thordarson advocated a cultic *Sitz im Leben*.[9] Based upon the widespread use of the credo and its literary context of covenant renewal (Exodus 32–34), he opts for the cultic setting.[10] Also following the prevailing theory of his day regarding an annual festival, Thordarson held that the credo's origins were in the annual covenant renewal festival.[11] He believed that the main function of the ceremony was the forgiveness of the nation's sins and contained "rites of penance." Therefore, the credo would be emphasized in the part of the ceremony where the nation asked for YHWH to forgive. Thordarson based his argument on the fact that credo shows up several times in laments. For example, the credo occurs in several lament psalms (79:8; 90:8; 69:5, 11; 130:3) and its original context of Exodus 32–34 contains all of the necessary elements of the Autumn Festival: ritualistic sin, prayers of intercession and humiliation.[12] These elements all point to the actual place within the festival that the credo held. Thordarson's work is important because he aggressively argues for not only a cultic *Sitz im Leben*, but even for the exact way in which the credo functioned within the annual Autumn Festival.

In 1963, Robert C. Dentan argued for a wisdom setting and origin in his article, "The Literary Affinities of Exodus XXXIV 6f."[13] Dentan's methodology centers on a lexical analysis of each of the different components of the passage. He believes that the only way to find the *Sitz im Leben* is "by examining the formula in isolation from its present context,

---

8. Ibid., 149.

9. Thordarson, "The Form-Historical Problem."

10. For the fullest formulation of the covenant renewal ceremony, see Mowinckel, *The Psalms in Israel's Worship*, 1:106–40.

11. Thordarson, "The Form-Historical Problem," 110.

12. Ibid., 126–54.

13. Dentan, "The Literary Affinities," 34–51.

and without regard merely to its possible relationship to the various documents of the Pentateuch and their redaction, in order to see whether or not its language, as well as its ideas, may not disclose so marked an affinity with one of the identifiable corpora of ancient Hebrew literature."[14]

Dentan's methodology has two steps. First, he seeks to find the historical context of Exod 34:6–7 by looking at the dependent passages such as the major parallels for an examination to see if they provide "any hints as to its age and origin."[15] Dentan's only conclusion from step one is that none of the literary contexts can be said to be earlier than Jeremiah. In the second step, Dentan analyzes each of the different phrases of the passage seeing in what other contexts the phrases appear.[16] This second step constitutes the bulk of Dentan's work as he methodically analyzes each of eight different parts of the passage.

From this work, Dentan finds five major conclusions.[17] First, he concludes that the passage was never a part of the J document and could not be from the earliest literary history of the texts. Second, it has no Deuteronomic element whatsoever. The basis for a Deuteronomic setting is based on its position in the Sinai narrative, not on a careful analysis of its constituent parts. Third, each part of the passage has strong wisdom affinities. "One can assert with confidence that the entire formula is a product of the School of Wise Men."[18] Fourth, the theological nature of Exod 34:6–7 should not be used to deter one from assigning a wisdom origin. Many wisdom writers (e.g., Prov 8:22–31) addressed theological as well as the normal ethical issues found in Wisdom Literature. Fifth, the scribes placed Exod 34:6–7 in important places to abate the "fanatical intensity" of the Deuteronomic literature with the "calm, rational and generous spirit manifest in the Orthodox Wisdom literature."[19]

The importance of Dentan's work comes in his thesis that Exod 34:6–7 has definite wisdom origins. Literarily, the passage appears in a strong covenantal context. In fact, Exodus 34 stands as one of the most important covenantal texts. It is the first instance of YHWH's renewal of

14. Ibid., 38.

15. Ibid.

16. Ibid., 39.

17. Ibid., 48–49.

18. Ibid., 48.

19. Ibid., 51.

the covenant after the people broke it. The text comes as a direct revelation of who God is and why God will forgive the people. Dentan's analysis argues that the language is representative of a wisdom context and not a covenantal one. This work asserts that in the final form of the text, there is evidence that the later wisdom tradition assimilated the earlier covenantal traditions to serve their ideology.

In 1989, Thomas B. Dozeman's "Inner-Biblical Interpretation of Yahweh's Gracious and Compassionate Character" compares the use of the credo in Jonah and Joel and concludes that the use of Exod 34:6–7 in these two prophets is inner-biblical exegesis of Torah renewal in the Twelve.[20] Dozeman's methodology is a hybrid between a form-critical analysis and a canonical analysis. He first looks for the similarities between Joel 2:1–17 and Jonah 3:1–4:11. Both contexts mention the Day of YHWH, both promise judgment from YHWH, and both call for Judah or Nineveh to repent with things like fasting and weeping but also with a change in character.[21] Next, Dozeman compares and contrasts the two different prophetic enunciations and finds that each interprets the other. The central theme holding together the two different uses of Exod 34:6–7 in these two prophets is that each is interpreting the "Torah passage" of Exodus 32–34. Joel argues for covenant renewal within the exclusive context of ancient Israel; Jonah postures for allowing the other nations into the exclusive covenant.[22]

The importance of Dozeman's article lies in the hybrid nature of his methodology. He uses form-critical methodology towards a canonical end. His comparison and contrast of different parts of the prophets' enunciation leads him back to theological issues present in Exodus 32–34. Furthermore, Dozeman's results lead him back to original passage of 34:6–7. He recognizes the inherent malleability of the text and that different communities could use the same text for a different end. His work also argues for an internal biblical dialogue between texts about important post-exilic problems.

In 1990, Hermannn's "Barmherzig und gnädig ist der Herr . . ." argues for a shift in the focus of the passage during the exile and after.[23]

---

20. Dozeman, "Inner-Biblical Interpretation," 207–23.

21. Ibid., 210.

22. Ibid., 220–23.

23. Spieckermann, "'Barmherzig,'" 1–18.

Spieckermann claims that the text in its place in Exodus 34 gives the core theological ideas whereby YHWH is to be known.[24] After a source-critical analysis of the different occurrences of the credo, Spieckermann also maintains that the merciful aspects became the dominant theological ideas for the community. The form of the credo was not finalized until after the exile. Originally, the "Gnadenformel" (Exod 34:6) was without the later portions of the passage (Exod 34:7). The late Deuteronomists developed 34:7 to explain the harshness of the exile. Furthermore, he argues that the passage may have originated in the cult, but later became "Bestimmung des theologischen Zentrums des Alten Testaments."[25] Spieckermann's work brings into the spotlight the development of the "Gnadenformel" in the exile and post-exile. What he calls the "mercy formula" becomes the most used portion of the larger passage. His work also highlights the importance of the theological ideas present for the formation of the canon and the formation of postexilic theology.

In 1995, Susan Pigott examined Exod 34:6–7. Her dissertation continues in the diachronic tradition and is the most thorough examination of the credo up to this point.[26] Pigott's work begins with an in-depth analysis of Exodus 32–34. In her analysis, she first addresses the issue of the connection of Exod 32:1–6 and 1 Kgs 12:28.[27] The Exodus passage describes Aaron's construction of the Golden Calf to appease the people, while the passage in 1 Kings describes the manufacturing of idols by Jeroboam to create rival worship centers in Bethel and Dan. She argues that the passage from Exodus 32 is the earlier of the two and that the Deuteronomists reworked the earlier texts to make Jeroboam the "villain of villains."[28] Pigott then turns to the historical origins of Exod 34:10–28. She argues, contra Wellhausen,[29] that the laws of the passage are most likely later and were crafted by the Deuteronomists or pre-Deuteronomists.[30]

---

24. Ibid., 8–9.

25. Ibid., 18.

26. Pigott, "God of Compassion and Mercy."

27. Ibid., 27–38.

28. Ibid., 36–38.

29. Wellhausen, *Die Composition des Hexateuchs*, 83–100.

30. Pigott, "God of Compassion and Mercy," 42–43.

Interestingly, Pigott does not treat the importance of discussing these diachronic issues on the interpretation of Exod 34:6–7. She simply moves on to a discussion of the *Sitz im Leben* of the passage. After a typical, but thorough form-critical analysis of the different parts of the passage, she weighs the different theories of origins (i.e., cultic setting, wisdom setting, or Deuteronomic setting) and opts for a fourth possibility—origination in an actual theophany of God to Moses.[31] She chooses this possibility because it can accommodate for the fact that parallels all seem to come from a common source, that the parallels are located in liturgical contexts and that the credo is integral to the story of Exodus 32–34. Pigott does not deny later emendation and use in the cult; she simply asserts that the passage originated with Moses' actual experience with the deity.

After this analysis of the origins of the credo, Pigott begins an extensive analysis of the major parallels in the Hebrew Bible which quote three or more elements of the original.[32] The results of her analysis show that the passage was manipulated and crafted in order to fit into its new context.[33] For example, Nahum emphasizes YHWH's judgment over YHWH's mercy in his indictment of the Ninevites (1:3), while Jonah bemoans YHWH compassion on the Ninevites (4:2). Pigott found that many of the parallels also cite or allude to the Exodus 32–34 narrative.[34]

Theological affirmations based upon her form critical analysis form the final chapter of her work. The primary focus of her work is a refutation of Marcion's views on tensions between the god of compassion and the god of wrath.[35] Pigott argues that the credo of Exod 34:6–7 offers a very balanced articulation of the character of YHWH. Even the passages that seem only to portray God as compassionate and loving are situated within contexts that balance this overemphasis on the compassionate attribute (or the other aspect was meaningless or irrelevant in the new context). In Pigott's opinion, the credo completely undermines any attempt to portray the Old Testament God as harsh, wrathful and completely unconnected to the merciful God of the New Testament.

---

31. Ibid., 89–111.

32. Ibid., 8. She analyzes Exod 20:5c–7, Num 14:18; Deut 5:9c–11; Joel 2:13b; Jon 4:2c; Nah 1:3; Pss 86:15; 103:8; 145:8; and Neh 9:17.

33. Ibid., 202–3.

34. Ibid., 202.

35. Ibid., 226–27.

Pigott's work is important for three reasons. First, her dissertation is the most comprehensive analysis of the passage of Exod 34:6–7 and the attendant literature up to this point. Pigott does a very good job of surveying the many different views and methodologies associated with the credo. Second, Pigott is the first to explore the relation of the two different aspects of the credo in its immediate context. Her analysis shows that if one aspect of the passage is missing or minimized in the parallels, then context provides a theological buffer to a one sided emphasis on YHWH's character. Third, her work also moves toward delineating the "major parallels" of the passage. She simply looks for parallels that use at least two or three elements of the parallels. While this methodology is simple it does address the parallels that one would intuit as major.

Matthias Franz completed the most recent diachronic approach to the credo.[36] After an extended history of scholarship, Franz moves into an analysis of ancient Near Eastern parallels to the language of divine grace and anger found in the passage. From this analysis, combined with a look at extrabiblical ancient Israelite prayers at Kuntillet ʿAjrud and Khirbet Beit-Lei he concludes that the concept of חנון in the ancient Near East was preexilic and faded in ancient Israel's theology of grace during and after the exile.[37] In the final section, he argues that 34:6–7 is neither Deuteronomic or Deuteronomistic, but rather that it has early wisdom origins and maybe the earliest creed found in the Old Testament.[38] Franz is the only interpreter to approach the text from a methodology based on ancient Near Eastern parallels. Franz's work gives added weight to the idea that the credo was early and that it had a widespread use.

Results of Diachronic Approaches

The results of the different diachronic approaches are varied and far from uniform. Source-critically, there is no general consensus about the dating of the original form of the credo. Most hold that the credo has ancient cultic origins. This theory arises from the fact that most of the quotations are in cultic settings and that the well known and widespread nature of the credo seem to point to cultic transmission.[39] Thorir Thordarson's

36. Franz, *Der barmherzige*.

37. Ibid., 93.

38. Ibid., 235–46.

39. Pigott, "God of Compassion and Mercy," 91.

conclusions have been implicitly accepted by most.[40] Another theory subverting the idea of cultic origins is Dentan's wisdom viewpoint (followed by Franz). Dentan's work finds its importance in showing that the credo does not contain cultic language. A third source theory is that the credo is Deuteronomic, emerging during the exile or after. Spieckermann, arguing from theological grounds, believes that the credo emerged to help explain the harshness of exile for the ancient Israelite people.[41] A final option is to allow, as does Pigott, for an origin within an actual experience with YHWH as the source.[42]

Correspondingly, there are no unified results from the form-critical analyses. Most hold that the verses represent an original unified tradition. Dentan, arguing from theological grounds, holds that the credo represents a "beautifully balanced statement with regard to the two most basic aspects of the character of God" that originated in the wisdom tradition.[43] He does not give a definitive date for what he considers the "Wisdom Tradition," but it does seem to be post-Deuteronomic. Another scholarly camp holds that 34:6 was early with 34:7 being a later addition. Scharbert's views represent this camp. He believes that the canonical form of the credo was postexilic as the harshness of 34:7 was added to the compassion of 34:6.[44] Another view is that certain phrases were added later to an earlier core tradition within 34:6–7. Katherine Doob Sakenfield holds this view arguing that the original tradition did not include "maintaining *chesed* to thousands" or "visiting the iniquity of the fathers upon the children and grandchildren unto the third and fourth generations."[45] She does not give a date of insertion or source of origin for the later additions.

40. E.g., Eissfeldt, *The Old Testament: An Introduction*, 72–73; Ahlström, *Joel and the Temple Cult*, 24–25; Beyerlin, *Origins and History*, 136.

41. Spieckermann, "Barmherzig," 3, did allow for an earlier, pre-exilic form of the passage, but held that the final form was exilic.

42. Pigott, "God of Compassion and Mercy," 110.

43. Dentan, "The Literary Affinities," 36.

44. Scharbert, "Formgeschichte," 133. For others who hold to this two part comparison, see Zobel, "חסד *Hesed*," 62–64, who argues that 34:6 represents the J tradition while 34:7 is a later E addition; Perlitt, *Bundestheologie im Alten Testament*, 214, also believes that the two verses are derived from separate traditions—34:6 only has parallels from the post-Deuteronomic tradition which shows that the verse originates in that tradition, while 34:7 is associated more closely with the Deuteronomic tradition.

45. Sakenfield, *The Meaning of* Hesed *in the Hebrew Bible*, 130–31.

No satisfactory consensus on diachronic issues has been found. Form-critically, the idea that the texts of 34:6–7 represent a unity is the most common view, but the view that holds that 34:7 was a later addition (Scharbert) and the view that small units of the final form were added also has followers (Sakenfield). Source-critically, most argue for or assume a cultic origin (Thordarson), while others argue for a wisdom origin (Dentan) or a post-exilic theological expression (Spieckerman).

I believe that the most that can be said about Exod 34:6–7 is that it represents the fullest expression of an ancient Israelite cultic formula with pre-exilic origins. I opt for this stance for the following reasons. First, the formulation expressed in Exod 34:6–7 is the most complete articulation in the Scriptures. It contains each of the core attributes used in the parallel constructions. Later exilic and postexilic prophetic interaction with the credo also testifies to the pre-exilic nature of the fullness of articulation. For example, both Jeremiah and Ezekiel give prophetic announcements that the theology of vertical retribution supported by the wrathful pole of the credo will be coming to an end (Jer 31:30; Ezek 18:2). Second, a cultic origin would explain the widespread use of the formula throughout the different times and canonical locations. Its parallels can be found in each section of the canon and in literary settings throughout Israel's history. Third, Dentan's argument for a wisdom setting unnecessarily separates cult and wisdom. Using ancient Near Eastern parallels to ancient Israelite wisdom literature, Leo Perdue argues that wisdom and cult are not necessarily separated.[46] After looking at Egyptian and Mesopotamian parallels, he looks to the Psalms where he finds significant interconnections between wisdom and the cult. Of special importance to Perdue is the idea of "order."[47] He uses this idea of order to show that the sages believe the cult to be an important element in maintaining order. He concludes, "As the traditional wise studied the various compartments of world order overseen by a just deity, they concluded that the cult had its own very important place within the structure of cosmic and social order."[48] Thus, Perdue shows that any type of contrast between sage and priest is unnatural and without textual warrant.

46. Perdue, *Wisdom and Cult.*

47. Ibid., 135.

48. Ibid., 225.

Synchronic Approaches

Scholarly analysis of the credo has also followed synchronic lines. As with the diachronic approach, much diversity exists in interpretation. Scholars use the text of Exod 34:6–7 to outline the fundamental characteristics of God, show an inherent tension in theological affirmations and even to show the artistic nature of hermeneutics. Several of these manifestations of synchronic analysis will now be explored.

In 1978, Phyllis Trible's *God and the Rhetoric of Sexuality* argues for the credo as a key text for understanding hermeneutics.[49] Trible uses the passage to show two things—the inability to systematize interpretation and the feminine characteristics of YHWH. Primarily, Trible shows how the text and its parallels are an example of inner-biblical interpretation.[50] She examines how the different parallels change the original to fit their narrative and sociological context. Her work shows how the parallels can be radically different from the original credo. After her brief examination, she concludes, "Interpretation, then, eschews systematizing."[51] Secondarily, Trible returns to the original text to examine the feminine characteristics of YHWH that it contains.[52] Her analysis hinges on the use of רחם, a key text both in 34:6–7 and in the Old Testament that denotes "compassion," but connotes "womb" and "uterus." The analysis of how רחם is used to convey a key attribute of YHWH leads her to proclaim, "The female organ becomes a theological and moral event."[53] Both of Trible's uses of the credo find theological and hermeneutical affirmations based on a synchronic, literary methodology. While her work is certainly not the most comprehensive synchronic analysis of Exod 34:6–7, it has been extremely generative for later scholarly contributions to hermeneutics, especially feminist hermeneutics.

---

49. Trible, *God and the Rhetoric of Sexuality*. Other important studies not covered in this section include Freedman, "God Compassionate and Gracious," 6–24, who provides a theological study of the passage; Smith, "The Reconciliation of the Moral Attributes of Yahweh as Revealed in Exodus 34:6–7," analyzes each of the different components of the credo in dealing with the tension between God's love and justice, but he offers no critical engagement with the text.

50. Trible, ibid., 1–4.

51. Ibid., 4.

52. Ibid., 31–59.

53. Ibid., 36.

In 1991, Thomas Raitt used the credo as a definitive example of why God forgives.[54] He explores the credo as a normative example of why God forgives and even states, "Exodus 34:6–7 is the closest thing to a normative statement on forgiveness within the Mosaic covenant tradition."[55] Raitt believes that the widespread use of the credo in the canon shows its normativity. This forgiveness is essential, because both the people and God knew that if God did not forgive, then the covenant would die.[56] After establishing the importance of the credo for the covenant, he then does an in-depth analysis of what he calls the "three love mountains" of the credo—חֶסֶד, רַחוּם and חַנּוּן. He concludes that the combination of these three strong terms that connote different aspects of love and forgiveness provides the "strongest imaginable statement of the motivation for forgiveness."[57] Raitt concludes with four affirmations about YHWH's forgiveness:[58]

1. Sin is taken seriously.

2. God is just.

3. God has such depth and richness of love that he can overcome sin with forgiveness.

4. God also will punish sin wherever and whenever it occurs.

Raitt's work is important for several reasons. First, he effectively and succinctly argues that Exod 34:6–7 is a central Old Testament text. His work helps to bring into the foreground the central nature of the credo in all areas of the canon. Raitt uses these observations to make his synchronic affirmations. Second, he shows the importance of the credo for later theological affirmations, both biblical and contemporary. Within the many different articulations of Exod 34:6–7 there are some key theological elements that the different rehearsals of the original show to be non-negotiable. Raitt emphasizes the centrality of these theological ideas for ancient Israel and the contemporary Church.

In 1993, Ralph Smith's *Old Testament Theology* became one of the very few Old Testament theologies to make significant use of the credo in

54. Raitt, "Why Does God Forgive?" 38–58.

55. Ibid., 45.

56. Ibid., 46.

57. Ibid., 51.

58. Ibid., 57–58.

shaping its theology.[59] Smith initially briefly discusses the formula itself and lists it among the "nonhistorical creeds" of ancient Israel along with the Shema (Deut 6:4), the First Commandment, and other "doxologies" (Amos 4:13; 5:8–9; 9:5–6; 1 Chr 29:10; Zech 12:1b).[60] Smith juxtaposes the credo with the historical credos such as von Rad's *kleine credo*. Smith also uses the credo in several of his discussions of the attributes of YHWH.[61] Finally, Smith also uses the passage in his discussion on the forgiveness of God. The credo plays a central role in his discussion of what forgiveness meant to the ancient Israelite. He argues that forgiveness cannot be defined as "remission of penalty" because "Remission of penalty requires an explanation and a justification. Remission of penalty can be good or bad. If it has no justification, it is immoral."[62] Instead of remission of penalty, Smith prefers to think of forgiveness as a "restoration of fellowship." This restoration of fellowship is what he believes the ancient Israelites were celebrating with the recitation of the credo. The importance of Smith's work lies simply in his heavy dependence on the credo for theological affirmations. He is one of the few Old Testament theologians to use the credo to this extent.

In 1997, Walter Brueggemann's *Theology of the Old Testament: Testimony, Dispute, Advocacy* used the credo as a standard to define his hermeneutic.[63] He makes special note of the fact that the theological attributes in 34:6–7 are adjectives. Brueggemann calls the passage "A Credo of Adjectives" that is full of core images the ancient Israelites used to describe YHWH.[64] He believes that the adjectives used in the "credo" formed a type of common stock from which the ancient Israelites could draw in their testimony. This "Credo of Adjectives" is especially appealing to Brueggemann because of the tension present between the "two different poles of the credo." He places added emphasis on the tension between the poles of the credo. The hermeneutic of his theology is based

---

59. Smith, *Old Testament Theology*.

60. Ibid., 83–84. Similarly Wright, *God Who Acts*, 85, notes, "The nearest the Bible comes to an abstract presentation of the nature of God by means of his 'attributes' is an old liturgical confession embedded in Exodus 34:6–7 . . . This confession is one of the very few in the Bible which is not a recital of events."

61. Smith, *Old Testament Theology*, 137, 165, 197, 199–201, 217, 225.

62. Ibid., 308.

63. Brueggemann, *Theology of the Old Testament*.

64. Ibid., 215–28.

upon a related theological tension that he finds between Israel's "core testimony" and "counter testimony."

Brueggemann does not mark the credo as normative because of any objective claims by ancient Israel, but simply "based upon characteristic usage."[65] He finds the credo used in Hymns of Praise (Ps 145:8), Prayers of Complaint (Ps 86:5, 15) and Daring Appeals (Numbers 14).[66] In each of these examples and in other uses of the credo throughout the Old Testament, Brueggemann observes a dramatic tension between outright, unfettered trust and pensive resistance. This theological tension is the focal point of most of his theological assertions. Brueggemann constructs a thoroughly postmodern theology which refuses objective theological statements, but affirms subjective statements held in dialogue with each other (thus his overall schema of testimony vis-à-vis counter-testimony). In fact after listing several statements predicated by the "credo of adjectives," he states that "Yahweh's incomparability is not in any one of these affirmations, but in the odd collage of all of them together."[67] Brueggemann's importance lies in the preeminent place that he gives the credo in constructing his hermeneutic. The theological tension between the two poles of the credo becomes the guiding framework through which he organizes what he believes are the core affirmations of the ancient Israelites.

In 2000, Harold Washington used the credo and its parallels as an example of how Christian nations should interact with Israel post-Shoah.[68] Washington seeks an interpretive posture toward Judaism that is not supersessionist, but is critically sensitive to the history of tension between the two religions. He begins this discussion with an analysis of the credo and its portrayal of YHWH as the gracious and compassionate God of Israel.[69] In this discussion, he pays special attention to the parallels of the credo found in the Hebrew Bible. Of special concern to him are the uses in Jon 4:2 and Joel 2:13 which open up YHWH's mercy to the nations. Washington believes that the church needs to begin identifying

---

65. Ibid., 221. Brueggemann makes a similar argument in his "Crisis-Evoked, Crisis-Resolving Speech," 95–105.

66. Brueggemann, *Theology of the Old Testament*, 218–21.

67. Ibid., 228.

68. Washington, "The Lord's Mercy Endures Forever," 135–45.

69. Ibid., 139–42.

itself with the nations rather than a "co-opted Israel."[70] He argues that this new understanding could lead the Church and Israel to begin to understand their relationship as one of mutual blessing that "could help move the church beyond mere tolerance of Jewish difference to genuine respect and appreciation."[71] Washington's hermeneutic uses the parallels of the credo in Jonah and Joel to reaffirm a latent relationship between Israel and the Church. He wants to recover an older model of interaction between Israel and the nations based on mutual blessing. Washington's use of the credo is important because he is one of the few to use the ancient credo to make concrete contemporary applications. Most important, he sees the key to uncovering the secret to finally finding peaceful and harmonious relations between the Church and Israel to be found in the credo and its parallels.

In 2002, Ruth Scoralick posited that Exod 34:6–7, as understood in the Golden Calf narrative of Exodus 32–34, can be a key to understand the Twelve.[72] Scoralick begins with a statement on her methodology and settles on approaching the text in a canonical context.[73] Next, Scoralick analyzes the credo within the Sinai pericope and concludes that the credo is central in the "Bundesbruchs" of chapters 32 to 34 and becomes a central idea that Israel reverted to during later crises.[74] Building on this foundation, she next moves to an examination of the Twelve. Scoralick concludes that the God speech of 34:6–7, understood in its context, is the key to understanding both the Twelve and its final form.[75] Scoralick's work is significant in that it approaches the credo from both synchronic and diachronic methods.

Rather like Washington, in 2003 Andreas Michel-Mainz argued that the credo is the theological center of Old Testament faith.[76] Michel-Mainz begins with a synchronic, canonical analysis 34:6–7 in the Torah, paying special attention to how the credo connects the Decalogue and the

---

70. Ibid., 142.

71. Ibid., 144.

72. Ruth Scoralick, *Gottes Güte und Gottes Zorn*.

73. Ibid., 7–9.

74. Ibid., 128–29.

75. Ibid., 204.

76. Michel-Mainz, "Ist mit der 'Gnadenformel,'" 110–23.

"Naming Passage."[77] He finds that there is no real connection of the credo to Genesis, but does not find a satisfactory answer to this dilemma. After this analysis of the credo in the Torah, he moves to a cursory discussion of the relationship between the credo and the rest of the Old Testament. From this analysis he believes that the placements in the Twelve serve as a final level of canonical emphasis.[78] Michel-Mainz concludes that the credo is certainly a key to Old Testament theology, but one which may not open all of the doors. Recognizing the wildly divergent nature of Old Testament texts, he concludes that the text can only be summarized by the text itself. The importance of Michel-Mainz's work is that it begins a synchronic canonical analysis over the whole canon. While he does focus mostly on the Pentateuch, he also briefly mentions the other two sections of the canon.

Results of Synchronic Analyses

The conclusions of synchronic analyses are as varied as those of the diachronic interpreters. They are used in both hermeneutical and theological ways. Washington sets up a modern two-step hermeneutic with his article arguing that the credo should be used to discover how ancient Israel related to the nations, so that the church might know how to relate to contemporary Israel. Trible and Brueggemann both use the credo to develop postmodern hermeneutics. Trible uses the credo to show the diversity of the different interpretations of the credo even within the canon. Brueggemann uses the credo similarly as a hermeneutical model for affirming the bipolar confession without resolving the tension. Some have also used the credo as a core text in affirming different aspects of their theological programs, either in one aspect such as forgiveness (Raitt) or in the core attributes of YHWH (Smith). Lastly, Michel-Mainz begins a brief canonical analysis of the credo calling it one of the keys to Old Testament theology.

Contrary to the results of the diachronic approaches studied, the synchronic results do not necessarily have to be mutually exclusive. For example, the hermeneutic programs of Trible and Brueggemann certain-

77. Ibid., 116–18. Michel-Mainz calls the appearance of the credo in Exodus 34 the "Naming Passage" because of the double YHWH that is given in the theophany before the attributes.

78. Ibid., 121.

ly allow for a wide variety of interpretations. Furthermore, the programs or Raitt and Smith use the credo to develop theological propositions that are not mutually exclusive. Smith would affirm Raitt contention that YHWH certainly forgives and Riatt would most likely affirm Smith's propositions. The preeminent place that the first five scholars have given to the credo shows that they would agree with Michel-Mainz's proposal that 34:6–7 is a key to Old Testament theology.

METHODOLOGY

The canonical methodology of this volume is marked by both synchronic and diachronic concerns. Synchronically, the study will focus on how Exod 34:6–7 functions within the final shape of the canon. Special attention will not only be given to the location of the parallels in the final form of the canon as a unifying feature, but also in the larger textual units, namely the Torah, the Twelve, and the Psalter. As noted above, scholars have studied Exod 34:6–7 and its parallels almost exclusively in isolation with no interest in their location in the larger narrative.[79] Diachronic approaches isolated the parallels so that lexical differences might be compared and contrasted in order to yield objective historical data; synchronic approaches isolated the parallels so that the lexemes might be mined for theological import. This work will explore this neglected area in the scholarly arena.

Synchronically, this aspect of the canonical methodology relates to Childs' "canonical analysis."[80] Childs is mainly concerned with the "shape" of the text and its larger contours. He looks for key words, phrases and themes that link together the smaller units (pericopes, chapters, books, etc.) with larger units. Childs' analysis has widespread popularity among contemporary scholars. For example, David Clines argues that the theme of the Pentateuch is the partial fulfillment of the promise to the patriarchs.[81] James Nogalski finds a variety of words and phrases that connect the different books of the Twelve that bring unity to its final

---

79. Interestingly, even Trible, who has championed rhetorical analysis, gave little attention to the larger narrative surrounding the passage (*God and the Rhetoric of Sexuality*, 1–30).

80. Childs, *Introduction to the Old Testament*, 69–80.

81. Clines, *The Theme of the Pentateuch*, 30.

shape.[82] Gerald Wilson argues that "dominant wisdom elements" provide shape to the final form of the Psalter.[83] The synchronic aspect of this work will combine all elements from all three of these different approaches, but will be especially sensitive to looking for repeated themes and phrases found in Exod 34:6–7 as a unifying feature of the canon.[84] Raymond van Leeuwen has explored the relation of the credo to the Twelve[85] and Michel-Mainz and Scoralick, as noted above, have briefly explored synchronic canonical issues, otherwise, no one has explored this area of scholarship.

Diachronically, this volume will focus on how the different communities crafted the original formulation of Exod 34:6–7 to fit a new context. This aspect of the work will focus on the "shaping" of the text. The analysis of the parallels of Exod 34:6–7 creates a special circumstance where both "shape" and "shaping" can be more fully appreciated; the privileged text is easily identifiable to help delineate issues of "shape," but the parallels are also different enough from the original that a definite "shaping" can be followed. James Sanders calls this canonical uncovering of "shaping" a diligent search for "the homegrown traditions and the borrowed ones."[86] What Sanders describes as the "homegrown traditions" are easily recognizable in this study. The parallels of Exod 34:6–7 are the core, "homegrown" traditions of the community. Finding the "borrowed"

---

82. Nogalski, *Literary Precursors to the Book of the Twelve*, esp. 24–27.

83. Wilson, "The Shape of the Book of Psalms," 138.

84. In this work, the tripartite shape of the Masoretic Text (MT) will be given preeminence, but the variations in the constellation of books in the Christian Old Testament and LXX will also be considered. While those who canonized the Christian Scriptures certainly did not invent a bipartite division of the Hebrew Bible, it seems that the tripartite division of the Tanakh was most likely the dominant shape of the Hebrew Scriptures by the first century BCE. For a fuller explication see the work of Roger T. Beckwith [*The Old Testament Canon of the New Testament Church and Its Background in Early Judaism*, who argues on titular grounds such as the appearance of "The Law of Moses, the Prophets, and the Psalms" (Luke 24:44) and "the Law, the Prophets and David" (4Q MMT) and argues on structural grounds such as the distribution of historical and non-historical books in chiastic formation in the Prophets and Writings. While Beckwith's affirmation that the canonical order was settled by the second century may be too strong (e.g., his assertion that the canonical order of the third section was established by this time [111]), his work does give ample evidence that the tripartite division was the most popular view.

85. Van Leeuwen, "Scribal Wisdom," 31–49.

86. Sanders, *Canon and Community*, 47.

traditions will be an exploration of the different ways that the community used the parallels.

Several other interpreters have also employed Sanders' style of canonical shaping. Nahum Sarna analyzes the different early literary traditions present in Psalm 89 and their manipulation into a new context to form Psalm 89.[87] Michael Fishbane surveys many different texts whose earlier literary forms were later reused in different contexts.[88] Scott Harris argues that the writer of Proverbs 1–9 makes several allusions to earlier texts, such as Genesis 37 and Jeremiah 7; 20, in an attempt to ground the authority of the later text in the tradition of the earlier texts.[89] Each of these interpreters addresses diachronic concerns as they analyze how earlier traditions are morphed and manipulated to fit new contexts and historical circumstances within Israel's history.

Michael Fishbane explores this phenomenon of diachronic inner-biblical exegesis in his discussion of *traditum* and *traditio*.[90] For Fishbane, the *traditum* represents the written texts handed down to a community, while the *traditio* are the modifications in the *traditum*. Fishbane uses the distinction to show that authority of the *traditum* is intimately connected to the *tradito*, that is the new articulations and manifestations do not undermine the established *traditum*, but bring the authority into the context of a new generation. In other words, the new context both shapes and is shaped by the tradition.

The most obvious objection to Sanders and Fishbane's methodology is that one must clearly identify the *traditum*, before the *traditio* can be explored. Lyle Eslinger argues against "inner-biblical exegesis" on these grounds.[91] He states, "If there is some [supposed] interconnection of separate texts, say a prophetic book and a pentateuchal book, any discussion of the supposed exegesis presumes a demonstrable precedence. You

---

87. Sarna, "Psalm 89," 29–46.

88. Fishbane, "Revelation and Tradition," 343–61.

89. Harris, *Proverbs 1–9*.

90. Fishbane, *Biblical Interpretation in Ancient Israel*, 5–19. Fishbane uses these concepts throughout the volume, but lays down the philosophical framework in these introductory pages. Fishbane builds upon the work of Douglas Knight, *Rediscovering the Traditions of Israel*, 5–20, although Knight is primarily concerned with oral traditions and their adaptations and modifications whereas Fishbane focuses on written traditions.

91. Eslinger, "Inner-Biblical Exegesis and Inner-Biblical Allusion," 48–56.

cannot discuss the qualities of diachronic interpretation in the detailed way that Fishbane does if you are not sure which way the literary connection points."[92] Eslinger instead proposes to use the terms "inner-biblical allusion" in place of "inner-biblical exegesis."[93] Inner-biblical allusion is defined by Eslinger as a literary analysis of how two similar texts interact without any preconceived ideas of historicity. That is "demonstrable precedence" is not made a priority, nor does it even come into the discussion. He allows the texts to control precedence. Texts are simply considered in their literary, canonical order. Eslinger's ideas of inner-biblical allusion are very similar to the synchronic canonical analysis of this work.

Eslinger's comments do not rule out inner-biblical exegesis as a possibility. In the discussion of historical-critical issues above, it was noted that most scholars conclude that the text of Exod 34:6–7 is the earliest form from which the other parallels are derived and has early cultic origins. For the purposes of finding the diachronic answers, this study will assume based on both theological and historical arguments that 34:6–7 is the earliest and most complete formulation of the ancient credo. A diachronic analysis of Exod 34:6–7 and its parallels will provide a clear exploration of how this text impacted the theology and textual production of the different post-exilic communities.

A second objection to Fishbane's methodology and intertextuality in general has been levied by literary critics. Julia Kristeva, who coined the term "intertextuality" has broadened the idea completely.[94] Kristeva argues that every text has been influenced by too many different "texts" for one text's influence to simply be analyzed. She famously asserts, "Any text is the absorption and transformation of another."[95] By this assertion, she means that all texts are inexplicably intertwined. The relationship between any two texts is far too complex simply to be able to see an easy 0-to-1 relationship such as usually posited in biblical studies. Instead, she has shown that all texts are interdependent and that meaning is continually being deferred.

Building upon the work of Mikhail Bakhtin, Kristeva leans heavily on the metaphor of the carnival to support her idea of intertextuality.

92. Ibid., 49.

93. Ibid., 56–58.

94. Kristeva, "Word, Dialogue and Novel," 48–49. See also Kristeva, *Desire in Language*.

95. Kristeva, *Desire in Language*, 66.

Bakhtin uses the idea of carnival to show the subversive nature of texts.[96] In the carnival, sociological classes are diffused and religious taboos are ignored as the participants celebrate the temporary suspension of the rules of life. "In the world of the carnival the awareness of the people's immortality is combined with the realization that established authority and truth are relative."[97] Kristeva builds upon Bakhtin's use of the carnival moving past the sociological and religious metaphors. She explores the idea that in the carnival the real and the acted are the same. She notes, "The scene of the carnival, where there is no stage, no 'theatre,' is thus both stage and life, game and dream, discourse and spectacle."[98] The same type of blurring occurs between the novel and the real. The carnival challenges Aristotle's 0–1 idea of differentiation and distinction in the same way that a novel can not be differentiated from its intertexts.[99] In short, Kristeva's program defines "intertextuality" as neither conscious influence nor intentional allusion, but as simply the eternally open-ended play between physical texts, cultural texts, and readers. Instead, intertextuality is impossible to delineate because every "text is constructed as a mosaic of quotations."[100] For diachronic inner-biblical exegesis, this idea of intertextuality undermines the interpreter's ability to delineate 0–1 equivocal relations between intertexts.

Theologian George Lindbeck introduces the idea of "intratextuality" as an alternative to intertextuality. Lindbeck describes the process of a text's influence upon a community as intratextuality.[101] Lindbeck's claims are important because he imagines a "privileged text" (in his case, the Bible) as providing the interpretive framework for a community. Lindbeck briefly interacts with what he calls "the deconstructionists" though not specifically Kristeva or Bakhtin. In enunciating the differences between the two different programs, he notes that the biggest difference lies in the weight given to the texts. He differentiates in this manner, "For the deconstructionists there is no single privileged idiom,

96. Bakhtin, "Carnival Ambivalence," 206–26. For a deeper explanation of his literary-theoretical analysis of the dialogic relationship between texts and communities, see Bakhtin, *The Dialogic Imagination*.

97. Bakhtin, "Carnival Ambivalence," 226.

98. Kristeva, "Word, Dialogue, and Novel," 49.

99. Ibid., 48–49.

100. Kristeva, *Desire in Language*, 66.

101. Lindbeck, *The Nature of Doctrine*, 136.

text, or text-constituted world. Their approach is *inter*textual rather *intra*textual—that is, they treat all writings as a single whole: all texts are, so to speak, mutually interpreting."[102] On the contrary, "In an intratextual religious or theological reading . . . there is a privileged interpretive direction from whatever counts as holy writ to everything else."[103] In this case, the text creates a world within which the community lives. While his work is helpful in seeing the impact of a text upon a community, it does little to show how the different postexilic communities shaped the texts. Lindbeck's work does give, however, a framework and modern day parallel for how Exod 34:6–7 could have impacted the communities of the post-exile. This framework shows that a text can both help form a community, but can also be formed by the community through the tradition.

Practically speaking, this methodology will consist of four steps. First, in canonical order each parallel will be examined, including historical-critical issues, in its immediate literary context. Second, each parallel's literary connection to Exod 34:6–7 will be analyzed. Special attention will be paid to the balance between the aspects of mercy and wrath in the parallels. Third, the function of the parallels within the larger canonical units will be examined. In this third step the major themes and ideas that the parallels highlight in that particular section of the canon will be examined. Fourth, the unifying function of the passage to the whole of the canon will be given special analysis, especially its relation of the movement toward YHWH's reign over the cosmos.

THESIS / OUTLINE

The Torah, the Twelve and the Psalter contain a number of parallels to Exod 34:6–7. This book will argue that the parallels of Exod 34:6–7 are strategically located in the Torah, the Twelve and the Psalter. These parallels mark a movement in the canon from particularism to universalism. In the Torah, the parallels all occur where the covenant is either threatened or being affirmed by the people. The parallels use aspects of both wrath and mercy to emphasize YHWH as Israel's intimate covenant partner. In the Twelve, the parallels mark YHWH's mercy and wrath on both Israel and the nations. In the Psalter, major parallels occur near the seams of

102. Ibid.

103. Ibid.

the last three books in psalms highlighting YHWH's kingship over the cosmos. These parallels suggest to readers a canonical movement toward YHWH as cosmic king, rather than simply Israel's covenant partner.

In the Torah, significant parallels occur in Exodus 20, Numbers 14 and Deuteronomy 5.[104] In each of these contexts, the covenant is either greatly endangered or being (re)affirmed.[105] The insertion of the parallels at these points marks these texts as important in the larger narrative. The inclusion of the parallels is especially important for recognizing the thematic unity that has recently been proposed by scholars.[106] This unity emphasizes the intimate covenant relationship between YHWH and Israel. The second chapter of the book will explore parallels found in the Torah.

In the Twelve, the parallels emphasize YHWH's relationship to the other nations. Joel 2, Jonah 4 and Nahum 1 all use the credo to highlight YHWH's interaction with the other nations. In addition to Scoralick's thesis, Raymond van Leeuwen has argued that the parallels used in the books of Hosea to Micah (in the MT) develop the issues of theodicy that the nation had to navigate after the judgments of 722 and 587.[107] The text is also used in Nah 1:3, and theological parallels can be found in the final six books. This chapter of the study will explore how the parallel in Nah 1:3 and the theological parallels in the other books indicate ways the nation dealt with the disappointment of the exile and after, again asserting that ancient Israel's hope rested in YHWH. The third chapter of this volume will show how the parallels in this section of the canon reveal YHWH's relationship to the other nations.

In the Psalter, parallels shows YHWH's kingship over the entire cosmos. Significant parallels occur in psalms that are close to the end of the last three books (86; 103; 145). The parallels in these psalms emphasize the ability of YHWH to save (86), the overwhelmingly positive character

---

104. By "significant," I mean parallels that contain three or more units of the original credo. The final section of this chapter will conduct a rhetorical outline of the credo and define what constitutes a unit. Pigott also only analyzes the significant parallels ("God of Compassion and Mercy," 8). While authorial intent cannot be proven, the presence of a significant parallel heightens the chance of authorial intent, and it also gives more data to compare to the original. From the perspective of the reader, these parallels are also easier for the reader to notice.

105. Brueggemann, "Crisis-Evoked, Crisis-Resolving Speech," 95–105.

106. E.g., Whybray, *The Making of the Pentateuch*.

107. Van Leeuwen, "Scribal Wisdom," 31–49.

of YHWH's reign (103), and the close connection of YHWH's compassion and reign (145). Attention will be given both to how the parallels fit into the individual psalms and then how each psalm fits into the different books of the Psalter. Recognizing the location of the parallels helps the reader to see the movement of the Psalter envisioned by Gerald Wilson, especially his "final wisdom frame."[108] The parallels highlight the Psalter's emphatic insistence that the ancient Israelites should trust in YHWH's reign over the cosmos rather than the local reign of earthly kings. The fourth chapter will examine the parallels in the Psalter.

The final chapter of this book will be a summary chapter dedicated to larger canonical concerns. For example, the function of the credo in the larger canon will be explored as well as any theological patterns in the manipulation of the credo throughout the canon. This chapter will conclude with prospects for further study.

PURPOSE

The purpose of this study will be threefold. First, no extensive research has been conducted on the appearance of the parallels in the final form of the text. This book will explore the location of the parallels within the final form and their contribution to a larger canonical movement toward YHWH's rule over the cosmos. Second, the location and manipulation of the parallels give clues to the theologies of the communities that created this final form. The many different articulations of Exod 34:6–7 in the parallels reveal variations in the theologies of the post-exilic communities. This diversity will be explored with special attention paid to theological issues. Third, the study will seek to show how the parallels bring unity to the final form of the text and enhance the narrative with the repetition of key themes and phrases.

EXCURSUS: THE TEXT OF EXODUS 34:6–7

This excursus will briefly examine the text of Exod 34:6–7 in isolation. This examination will be brief as there are several in depth analyses of the text available and each parallel will receive attention.[109] Rhetorically,

---

108. Wilson, *The Editing of the Hebrew Psalter*; Wilson, "Shaping the Psalter," 72–82.

109. For the most recent, see Pigott, "God of Compassion and Mercy," 68–85; Franz, *Der barmherzige*, 111–53; and Scoralick, *Gottes Güte*, 77–83.

the text can be divided two ways. The most popular path that interpreters follow is to divide the text into two competing theological affirmations or poles. These two poles are joined by an adversative *vav* that highlights the difference between the merciful God and the wrathful God, with the rhetorical weight on the side of the merciful attributes.

> YHWH, YHWH,
> The compassionate and gracious God,
> slow to anger and great in loving kindness and faithfulness,
> extending loving kindness to the thousandth generation, and
> taking away iniquity, transgression and sin.

However,

> he will surely not acquit the guilty,
> visiting the iniquity of the parents on the children
> and their children
> unto the third and fourth generation.

This theological juxtaposition has provided enormous stimulation for both biblical and modern interpreters.

Another rhetorical way of dividing the text is as follows:

(A) YHWH, YHWH

(B) Compassionate and gracious God,
  Slow to anger
  Great in loving kindness and faithfulness.

(C) Extending loving kindness to the thousandth generation (a)
  Taking away iniquity, transgression and sin (b)
  However, he will surely not acquit the guilty (b')
    visiting the iniquity of the parents on the children and (a')
    their children unto the third and fourth generation.

Stanza A is governed by the double giving of the divine name. A threefold affirmation of YHWH's merciful attributes marks Stanza B. The final stanza is composed of a chiasm that highlights the vertical nature of YHWH's judgment. The credo pairs *a* and *a'* in such a way to accentuate the fact that YHWH's judgment is not contained within one generation. God's mercy or wrath overflows spilling out from one generation to the next. This vertical aspect is mediated by the fact that God's mercy extends to thousands of generations, while his mercy is only doled out to the fourth. Furthermore, the merciful attributes of YHWH (*b*) are rhetorically three times stronger than its wrathful counterpart (*b'*). This tripartite division of the credo also emphasizes YHWH's mercy, but not at the expense of YHWH's ability to unleash wrath.

These two different ways of reading the credo do not have to be read in an either/or fashion. The two different ways of reading the credo can complement each other. In either case, the merciful attributes are given preeminence, while the wrathful attributes are second in both number and place. Ancient Israelites believed the chief characteristic to be mercy, rather than wrath.

Grammatically, the credo is made up of nine separate clauses. A lexical analysis of these clauses will end this chapter.

יהוה יהוה —*YHWH, YHWH*

This is the only occurrence of the double name to be found in the Hebrew Bible, in fact the construction is so unusual that the LXX omits one of the names. Cassuto translates the second יהוה as a verbal, "YHWH, he is Lord" which he believes is a summation of the theology found in the previous section.[110] Pigott opts for a simple translation of "YHWH, YHWH" based upon the accents in the MT.[111]

אל רחום וחנון —*Compassionate and Gracious God*

These three words occur together only in Exod 34:6, Neh 9:31, Psalm 86:15 and Jonah 4:2 although sometimes in different order. The phrase is similar to the titular phrases associated with El. In fact, Marvin Pope has argued that the phrase may have originally been associated with El, but was later assigned to YHWH.[112] As noted by Trible, רחום denotes compassion, but is related to the female womb. This word shows that YHWH's love for Israel is as intense as a mother's toward her child. Raitt believes that חנון conveys the idea of a superior granting mercy toward an inferior.[113] Ap-Thomas concludes that חנון is an aspect of YHWH's צדקה and that YHWH will simply grant mercy to whom he sees fit—it

---

110. Cassuto, *A Commentary on the Book of Exodus*, 439.

111. Pigott, "God of Compassion and Mercy," 71.

112. Pope, *El in the Ugaritic Texts*, 25.

113. Raitt, "Why does God Forgive?" 51.

is an aspect of his sovereignty.[114] These two terms categorically emphasize the fact that YHWH will act positively toward Israel, even as a mother acts toward a child and, yet as undeserving, and with the authority of a superior toward an inferior.

ארך אפים—*Slow to Anger*

This idiom could be literally translated "long of nose" and stems from the fact that when one gets angry, one's face burns. It is used to show that YHWH "is not easily angered" by the people. YHWH's long nose means that he is slow to anger. The idiom occurs in every significant parallel of the credo except those associate with the Decalogue, which most likely stems from the emphasis in the legal passages on YHWH's punishment on those who disobey. YHWH's long nose is simply a negative restatement of the previous phrase. YHWH's mercy will not be quickly taken from the people.

ורב־חסד ואמת—*Great in Loving Kindness and Faithfulness*

This phrase is dominated by the complex and multifaceted חסד.[115] Nelson Glueck produced the first extensive treatment of this central Old Testament concept where he demonstrated that חסד signifies covenantal and mutual obligations.[116] Katherine Doob Sakenfield later argued that Glueck's hypothesis was flawed concluding instead that "*Hesed* is not a legal right, but a moral right and as such can also be a gift."[117] She believes that its origin was mercy, not obligation. Most recently, Gordon Clark has disagreed with Sakenfield and argued that the concept does imply "mutual, bilateral commitment."[118] The word is notoriously difficult to translate and many translators simply transliterate the Hebrew into English. It most likely implies kindness granted to someone with whom one is in a relationship with, thus "loving-kindness."

---

114. Ap-Thomas, "Some Aspects of the Root HNN in the Old Testament," 140–41.

115. For an extensive summary of scholarship, see Pigott, "God of Compassion and Mercy," 75–76.

116. Glueck, Hesed *in the Hebrew Bible.*

117. Sakenfield, *The Meaning of* Hesed *in the Hebrew Bible,* 2–3.

118. Clark, *The Word* Hesed *in the Hebrew Bible,* 261.

חסד along with אמת may form a hendiadys, representing a single concept of "faithful loving kindness."[119] אמת, however, is missing in most of the significant parallels which shows that the earliest interpreters did not consider the two terms to have such a deep connection. Stated simply, the terms together convey the idea that YHWH can be trusted to uphold his side of the relationship with the people. It is a positive statement again after the negative, "Not easily angered."

נצר חסד לאלפים—*Extending Loving Kindness to the Thousandth Generation*

This phrase begins a string of phrases that start with participles. The verb נצר is used, Dentan argues, instead of the more usual עשה to show that YHWH's extension of loving kindness is not merely habitual, but flows from the essence of his nature.[120] This extension overflows from generation to generation. אלפים could either be translated "to thousands" (e.g., KJV, NIV, NJB and NLT) or "to the thousandth generation" (e.g., JPS, NAB, NRSV, and TNK). I opt for understanding the noun as a temporal marker ("thousandth generation"), rather than simply a statement of breadth ("thousands of people") because of the parallel with the generational wrath expressed in the final phrase of the credo.

נשא עון ופשע וחטאה—*Taking away Iniquity, Transgressions, and Sin*

The second participial phrase continues the affirmation of YHWH's positive attributes. While נשא literally means to "lift away or carry," here it takes on the idea of forgiveness.[121] YHWH forgives the sin by taking it away. The three terms used for sin (עון ופשע וחטאה) can be taken as either three different aspects of sin ("iniquity, transgression and sin") or as representing the totality of any kind of sin. The idea here is most likely that YHWH is able to forgive any kind of sin that the people might commit.[122]

119. E.g., Cassuto, *Exodus*, 439; Sarna, *Exodus*, 216.

120. Dentan, "The Literary Affinities," 45.

121. Cf. Gen 50:17; Josh 24:19; 1 Sam 15:25; Job 7:21; Isa 2:9; Hos 1:6.

122. For similar interpretations, see Cassuto, *A Commentary on the Book of Exodus*, 440; Pigott, "God of Compassion and Mercy," 78; Westermann, *The Living Psalms*, 94–95.

ונקה לֹא יְנַקֶּה—*However, He Will Surely Not Acquit the Guilty*

This third verbal phrase begins the enunciation of YHWH's wrath upon the unrighteous. An imperfect follows an infinitive absolute and gives emphasis to the verbal root נקה which means to "pardon." The phrase emphasizes the fact that YHWH will in no way pardon those who are guilty which seems to stand in stark contrast to the merciful aspects related in the first half of the credo.

פֹּקֵד עֲוֹן אָבוֹת בָּנִים וְעַל־בְּנֵי בָנִים—*Visiting the Iniquity of the Parents on their Children and Their Children*

This verbal phrase again takes up the participial form to emphasize the repeated action of YHWH's visitation. פקד denotes "visiting" and does not necessarily imply a negative context (cf. Gen 50:24–25; Ruth 1:6; Ps 8:4; Jer 15:15), but in this context it is negative as YHWH is bringing his judgment.[123] YHWH returns the consequences of the sin upon the parent's children and their children.

עַל־שִׁלֵּשִׁים וְעַל־רִבֵּעִים—*To the Third and Fourth Generation*

This final phrase intensifies the degree and extent of YHWH's punishment. Sarna notes that this phrase is most often used to describe the context of a divine reward for righteousness, both in the Bible and Aramaic inscriptions.[124] Here the phrase is turned around to show that wrath is as likely to follow one as blessing. In the context of the credo, it stands in stark contrast to the אֲלָפִים which experience YHWH's loving kindness.

This very brief summary of the credo outlines the major contours and shape of the text. Intensity characterizes each section. The first half adamantly declares that YHWH will forgive any kind of sin and that his loving kindness reaches out to thousands. At the same time, the second half warns that in no way will YHWH's mercy be taken advantage of—that each guilty party will be punished. Furthermore, in the same way that the loving kindness reaches to thousands, God's wrath will be

123. Hamilton, "פקד," 731–32.

124. Sarna, *Exodus = [Shemot]*, 111. See Gen 50:23; 2 Kgs 10:30; Job 42:16; *Ancient Near Eastern Texts*, 561, 661.

extended for three to four generations on those who disobey. The rich, contrasting imagery provided a deep pool from which the later writers of Scripture could draw.

CONCLUSIONS

This first chapter of this book has covered many foundational things in relation to the text of Exod 34:6–7. A history of scholarship was outlined following both synchronic and diachronic genealogies. Regarding diachronic studies, it was noted that no scholarly consensus exists, but I opted for a pre-exilic cultic setting for the origin of the credo. Synchronic approaches have also produced varied results, but these results are not necessarily contradictory. A statement on my methodology was also given where I revealed that this study will use both synchronic and diachronic data to show an overall canonical movement toward YHWH as king over the whole earth. Finally, the chapter ended with a very brief analysis of the contours and lexemes of the credo that showed the rich language and contrasting imagery that inspired later interpreters.

2

Parallels of Exodus 34:6–7 in the Torah

INTRODUCTION

Exodus 34:6–7 or its parallels occur four times in the Torah. This chapter will argue that the parallels occur in places where the covenant is either greatly endangered or being (re)affirmed. In the Decalogue of Exodus 20, a parallel is located in the giving of the second commandment as a reason why ancient Israel should not worship idols or images. In Numbers 14, Moses recited the credo to incite YHWH's pride so that the Israelites might be spared. In the Decalogue of Deuteronomy 5, a parallel is again found in the rehearsal of the second commandment.

All four of the appearances, including Exod 34:6–7, are in texts that highlight YHWH's intimate relationship with Israel. Exodus 20 records the initial giving of the Sinai Covenant and the "Ten Words" of the covenant. Exodus 34 contains the account of YHWH and Moses' interaction after the apostasy of the Golden Calf. In this literary context, the credo is given as a reason why YHWH will forgive the nation. Numbers 14 catalogues the second major apostasy of the ancient Israelites. In this narrative, Moses convinces YHWH not to wipe out the people by quoting the attributes given to him in Exodus 34. Deuteronomy 5 contains the final significant parallel to the credo in the Pentateuch. This parallel occurs in the rehearsal of the Ten Commandments as the people reaffirm the covenant as they prepare to enter the Promised Land.

This chapter will argue that parallels of the credo occur at significant junctures in the narrative, highlighting YHWH and Israel's relationship as intimate covenant partners. As noted in the introductory chapter, each parallel will be assessed in canonical order in four distinct steps. First, the diachronic issues associated with each parallel will be addressed. Second, an examination of the parallels' literary connection to Exod 34:6–7 will be addressed. Third, the function of the parallel within the larger pericope will be examined. Last, the chapter will end with an analysis of how the parallels function within the Torah.

EXODUS 20

Diachronic Issues

The diachronic issues of Exodus 20 and Deuteronomy 5 will be considered together because of their close connection. Progress in Decalogue studies has been made over the last century in both form-critical studies and redaction-critical studies.[1] Sigmund Mowinckel first proposed a cultic *Sitz im Leben* for the Decalogue in 1927.[2] This stance is not surprising considering his insistence that the entire Psalter was cultic. More specifically, he held that the Decalogue was used as an entrance liturgy during the great New Year's Festival.[3] The people would declare their purity by affirming their keeping of the commands. The Decalogue's final modification came by the hand of Isaiah's disciples who also used the commands as a type of entrance liturgy into their circle.[4]

Albrecht Alt's essay "Origins of Israelite Law," first published in 1934, disagreed with Mowinckel's conclusions.[5] In this essay, Alt distinguished between two types of biblical law, casuistic and apodictic, based upon evidence from other ancient Near Eastern cultures, especially Hittite law codes. Alt defines casuistic law as conditional and dependent upon specific legal cases.[6] These case laws are introduced by the formula "If you . . ."[7] Alt's second category of apodictic describes unconditional

---

1. For a survey see Stamm and Andrew, *The Ten Commandments in Recent Research*; Nielson, *The Ten Commandments in New Perspective: A Traditio-Historical Approach*; Johnstone, "The 'Ten Commandments'" 453–61; "The Decalogue and the Redaction of the Sinai Pericope in Exodus," 361–85.

2. Mowinckel, *Le Décalogue*.

3. Ibid., 114–21.

4. Ibid., 156–62.

5. Alt, "The Origins of Israelite Law," 101–71.

6. Ibid., 112–32.

7. Ibid., 113–14.

commands marked by the imperative form "You shall . . ."[8] He believes that apodictic laws are different in both form and content from the laws of ancient Israel's neighbors. He sees such a sharp distinction that he believes that only YHWH could have demanded such a legal system.[9] Furthermore, the Decalogue provided the prototypical example of the form of apodictic law. Contra Mowinckel, Alt held that the *Sitz im Leben* of the commandments could be found in the Feast of Tabernacles held in the Sabbath Year, but ultimately with "no unassailable proof that the Decalogue was the prototype of the whole literary category of apodictic law. . . the relationship to one another in time and place of origin of all the extant lists of apodeictic law is still unknown."[10] Alt's theories gained a significant following and many still follow his schema to some degree.[11]

George Mendenhall's "Covenant Forms in Israelite Tradition" furthered the connection between ancient Israel's laws and its ancient Near Eastern environment postulated by Alt.[12] Mendenhall's work articulated a close connection between ancient Israel's law and Hittite suzerainty treaties. Furthermore, Mendenhall made the idea of covenant the fundamental aspect of the religion of the people, especially the early tribal federation.[13] After listing the key components and structure of Hittite treaty texts, he asserts that the Decalogue and Joshua 24 are the two fullest examples of an ancient Israelite treaty.[14] Mendenhall found both political and religious freedom in the tribal covenant; the Decalogue formed a central text around which the tribes found centralization in their allegiance to YHWH.[15] Allegiance to YHWH also meant that the

8. Ibid., 133–71.

9. Ibid., 141.

10. Ibid., 165–68; quotation from 168.

11. For a survey of Alt's work and especially the Decalogue's connection to Mesopotamian law, see Van Seters, *A Law Book for the Diaspora*, 8–19.

12. Mendenhall, "Covenant Forms in Israelite Tradition," 50–76. See also Mendahall's "Ancient Oriental and Biblical Law," 26–46. For a similar view, see Baltzer, *The Covenant Formulary*. Later, Dennis McCarthy does an extensive analysis of the Decalogue's participation in the Hittite Treaties [*Treaty and Covenant*, 243–56]. McCarthy concludes that in spite of several missing features of the traditional form, the Decalogue can be characterized as a covenant form because the "ritual looms larger than the verbal" (256).

13. Mendenhall, "Biblical Law," 28–29.

14. Mendenhall, "Covenant Forms in Israelite Tradition," 57–63.

15. Ibid., 63.

people did not have to give their allegiance to any other political power, either Moses or another local power.

The next major form-critical work to tackle the origins of the Decalogue was Erhard Gerstenberger's dissertation *Wesen und Herkunft des 'apodiktischen Rechts'*.[16] He first deconstructs Alt's categories by showing that the Decalogue does not contain "law" in that it has no consequences; rather, it should only be thought of as prohibition.[17] Gerstenberger also differs from the form-critical interpreters before him in that he finds its *Sitz im Leben* in the family life of ancient Israel, not in the cult.[18] He bases this assumption on the basic form of eight of the commands, "You shall not . . . ," and holds that this form should be traced back to its original setting in family life. As parents instruct their children with the "You shall not . . . ," these commands eventually became part of ancient Israel's religious life.[19] Gerstenberger argues that the familial form of the commands proved it to be rooted in clan life, not in cultic life. Later professional priests and prophets adopted the texts and traditions of the family to solidify the authority of the cult. Thus, the final form of the Decalogue is a late development, not earlier as many have espoused.

Since Gerstenberger's dissertation, issues relating to the redaction of the Decalogue have risen to the surface showing the Ten Words to be a product of multiple layers of emendations and additions. Scholarship can be divided into two separate camps—those that espouse the primacy of the Exodus 20 version and those that hold that the Decalogue of Deuteronomy 5 came first. Eduard Nielson represents the standard traditio-critical evaluation of the Decalogue that holds to the primacy of Exodus 20.[20] He believes that the Exodus version is the earlier of the two extant biblical versions, but that "at no point have we concealed the fact that on form-critical grounds we have had to accept that the Decalogue, even in its earliest form in Ex. 20, has come down to us in a form which has been greatly worked over."[21] The current form most likely can be dated

16. Gerstenberger, *Wesen und Herkunft*.

17. Ibid., 55–61.

18. Ibid., 110–17.

19. For a summary of Gerstenberger's evolutionary system of ancient Israelite religion, see his *Theologies in the Old Testament*.

20. Nielson, *Ten Commandments in a New Perspective*.

21. Ibid., 43.

sometime between 622 and 560.[22] Before this time, he believes that commands I–IV are marked by YHWH's jealously, which would have been popular before settlement into the land.[23] After this step, he suggests that an early form of the Decalogue served as a basic law for the Northern kingdom and was the fundamental principle upon which all judgments were made.[24] For Nielson, the Northern kingdom was the probable place of origin of the earliest form of the Decalogue.

Henning G. Reventlow offers a slightly more nuanced version of Nielson's redactional program.[25] He sees four stages in the production of the Decalogue. The first stage was made up of two separate series of apodictic laws from Torah material and other places. These two were combined to form the second stage which resulted in the original form of the Decalogue. This original form was used in a cultic proclamation of the law. The third stage came about as the priestly writers expanded the laws in places that needed further clarification. The fourth stage was the result of Deuteronomic sermonic expansion. The Exodus and Deuteronomy versions of the Decalogue both exhibit different versions of this fourth stage, but the Deuteronomy version is later as it exhibits more expansion. In sum, those who hold to the primacy of Exodus 20 do so based upon the numerous additions of the Deuteronomy version. This camp holds that the expansions represent a development of the text.

Norbert Lohfink occupies a central position between the two opposite viewpoints. He does not look for the earlier of the two versions, but sees a common text behind the two which was restructured into the two current versions of Exodus 20 and Deuteronomy 5; his reconstruction imagines a rather different progression of the texts.[26] Lohfink begins with the premise that since the Decalogue was an "official" text it would have been very stable and could not have undergone multiple changes and alterations (contra Reventlow).[27] In place of multiple changes, he advances the position that one major change occurred which made the Sabbath

---

22. Ibid., 119.

23. Ibid., 120. From this point on, the commands will be designated by their corresponding Roman numeral.

24. Ibid., 137.

25. See Reventlow, *Gebot und Predigt im Dekalog*, 93–95 for an outline of his schema. It is from these pages that this summary is taken.

26. Lohfink, "The Decalogue of Deuteronomy 5," 248–64.

27. Ibid., 251.

command the principal command of the Decalogue. He finds a chiastic structure in the final form of the text that emphasizes Sabbath.[28] In his discovery of the Sabbath chiasm, he is able to delineate the material added to make the chiasm work. He then uses this information to formulate a methodology for finding other editorial clues for the theology of the P redactor. His last assertion is that this Sabbath Decalogue replaced an earlier version of the Decalogue already present in Exodus.[29] He argues that most differences between the two Decalogues can be traced to this one large wholesale change because the needs of the exilic people necessitated the emphasis on Sabbath keeping.[30]

William Johnstone offers possibly the most nuanced version of a redactional theory based upon the primacy of the Deuteronomy version.[31] He begins with the premise that the P-edition (Exodus 20) emphasizes the presence of God, holiness and realized eschatology while the D-edition (Deuteronomy 5) emphasizes firstborn, covenant and eschatology.[32] He argues that these different contours can be seen in the text. From these premises, Johnstone believes that the version of the Decalogue found in Deuteronomy is the earliest. He also believes that one could find a "D-version" of the Exodus Decalogue by removing the "retrospect" features of the current Deuteronomy Decalogue, such as "as the LORD your God commanded you."[33] Thus one can see that the major revision of the P-editor was the addition of the motivation for keeping the Sabbath. "The D-version of Exodus provides the exilic account of Israel's origins."[34] This D-version should not be used to provide historical data, but understood as an ideal, eschatological statement. Understanding the Decalogue in this ideal context explains the absence of social concerns present in the prophets, such as the care for widows and orphans. The later P-version was written after the return to the land.[35] For Johnstone, the major differences between the D and P versions can be seen in the fourth commandment. For D, it was a reminder of the freedom from

28. Ibid., 254.

29. Ibid., 261.

30. Ibid., 263.

31. Johnstone, *Exodus*.

32. Ibid., 96–98.

33. Ibid., 97.

34. Ibid.

35. Ibid., 98.

slavery for the exiles and "its observance provides a proleptic experience of eschatological return to the freedom of the promised land"; for P, it is participation in the ideals of creation when all things were in order and it is a look forward to the redistribution of Jubilee when all of creation will be rightly ordered again.[36]

Frank-Lothar Hossfeld also argues for the primacy of the Deuteronomy version of the Decalogue.[37] Hossfeld argues that the D version of the Decalogue is the earlier of the two versions. The version found in Exodus 20 is actually a P revision of an earlier D Decalogue which the P redactor first placed in Exodus 20. Hossfeld's methodology is focused on a formal comparison between the two versions of each commandment. For example, Hossfeld argues that Deuteronomy's I and II should be understood as one commandment because לֹהֶם must refer back to the gods of I and the idols of II; the Exodus Decalogue separates the two commands and adds "image *and* any likeness" as the grammatical antecedent of לֹהֶם.[38] Hossfeld also bases his argument on a comparison of both versions of II. In the Exodus version, the echo of 34:6–7 reads, "visiting the iniquity of the fathers upon the children, *that is*, upon those of the third generation" while the Deuteronomy version is "visiting the iniquity of the fathers upon the children, *and* upon those of the third generation." In the difference Hossfeld finds two different ways of counting the father in the generations.[39] The Exodus version excludes the father, so that the third generation is the great-grandson; the Deuteronomy version includes the father, so that the third generation is the grandson. Hossfeld argues that an earlier way of understanding the generations included the father (cf. Exod 34:7; Job 42:16), while the later version excludes the father (cf. Gen 15:16; Exod 6:13; 2 Kings 10:30). Hossfeld's other arguments are based on similar comparisons between the commandments.

Hossfeld's ideas have been critiqued heavily by later scholars in spite of his creativity.[40] Most criticisms rest on the fact that the Decalogue of Exodus is significantly shorter than the Deuteronomy version. These

---

36. Ibid.

37. Hossfeld, *Der Dekalog*.

38. Ibid., 21–26.

39. Ibid., 26–32.

40. Lang, "Neues über den Dekalog," 58–65; Levin, "Der Dekalog am Sinai," 165–91; Graupner, "Zwei Arbeiten zum Dekalog," 308–29; Weinfeild, *Deuteronomy 1–11*, 290–91.

scholars hold that these revisions show that the Deuteronomy version expanded the earlier Exodus version. Other than the aetiologies associated with the Sabbath commandment, the Exodus version only contains two semantically significant additions (both *vav*) in II and X.[41] Other criticisms leveled against Hossfeld are based on the thematic differences between the two Decalogues. For example, Graupner argues that the position of the wife in Deuteronomy's X as set apart from the household ("You shall not covet your neighbor's wife . . ." vis-à-vis "You shall not covet your neighbor's house . . ."), shows that the Exodus version is earlier as the position of the wife would not have deteriorated from the earlier to the later.[42] The wife is given a privileged position over the rest of the household in the Deuteronomy version, while she is simply considered part of the household in Exodus. Graupner sees no way that the wife's position would have fallen over time.

In spite of these objections, I believe the Exodus version to be later. The key to dating the two Decalogues resides in the expansion of the Sabbath commandment. In Deuteronomy 5, the remembrance of the Exodus is given as the reason for the keeping of the Sabbath— "you were slaves in Egypt." The idea of the Exodus was a strong one during the exile as God's people looked back to remind themselves of God's future provision. The rehearsal of the commandments in this context is a dramatic affirmation that their God will once again restore them to an ideal state of freedom. In Exodus 20, the reason for the keeping of the Sabbath is based upon the creation theology of the Priestly writer who made the changes sometime shortly after the exile. The creation and blessing of the seventh day serves as the prime motivation for the Sabbath's remembrance. These two different motivations for keeping Sabbath, more than principles which assert that shorter texts are older, show the more reliable dates of the two texts.

The results of diachronic exegesis are threefold. First, the commandments had their origin in the household (following Gerstenberger) before they were later incorporated into the official cultic religion. These early commands were most likely found in a very simple form, termed the "Urdekalog" by some.[43] The early form was mostly uniform, terse negative

41. Johnstone, "Decalogue and the Redaction of the Sinai Pericope," 368.

42. Graupner, "Zwei Arbeiten zum Dekalog," 321.

43. For a typical reconstruction of the *Urdekalog* see Johnstone, *Exodus*, 91–92 and Stamm and Andrew, *Ten Commandments*, 18–19.

commands. This development explains both the wisdom and cultic characteristics of the commandments. In this early form the commands were not necessarily linked together, but given only as the impartation of the household wisdom demanded it. In like manner, the first and second commands were originally differentiated from each other and then combined at a later time.[44] Second, these commands exhibited significant redaction and expansion into their present form. Unfortunately, reconstructions of the expansion are directly related to a reconstructed history of ancient Israel. All presuppose to some extent the Wellhausean reconstruction of ancient Israelite history. For example, Mendenhall's ideas of law relate to covenant and Gerstenberger places the commands in the clan setting. Every interpreter crafts ideas about the Decalogue to fit a reconstruction. Third, the parallel of Exod 34:6–7 was added to II as the cult appropriated the early, terse command to not worship idols or images. The command was subsidized theologically by insertion of the credo. The later addition gave theological weight as the cult emphasis sought to end the decentralizing effect of multiple idol worship. Fourth, the current form of the Deuteronomy version of the Decalogue most likely originated during the exile as part of a great theological vision by Dtr. The vision was recrafted in the P version of the Decalogue found in Exodus.

The credo as it now stands in this version of the Decalogue in Exodus is a vision of a future community that will no longer be subjected to the disorder of the foreign gods. The Decalogue envisions a future time in which YHWH's people will no longer have to worship the dreadful idols. The people would have been expected to imagine a great future time when YHWH's reign would be realized again and creation order would be reestablished. The emphasis on YHWH's wrath in this version of the credo (discussed below) would have reminded the people that they are expected to be obedient in this radical new vision of life.

Participation in Exodus 34:6–7

The parallel of Exod 34:6–7 found in Exodus 20 is a unique and interesting quotation of the original. The parallel contains the following connections with the original. From the compassionate pole, "giving loving kindness to the thousandth generation" is the only aspect quoted. Of

---

44. Childs, *The Book of Exodus*, 407.

YHWH's wrathful characteristics, "visiting the iniquity of the parents on the children and their children unto the third and fourth generation" is rehearsed.

There are three significant changes in the credo, however. In addition to a contraction of the remainder of other parts of the credo, the most significant change in this parallel is the reversal of the aspects of compassion and wrath. In association with the Decalogue, the wrathful aspects are recounted first, and then the compassionate acts of YHWH. Second, the overall balance of the credo has shifted as the weight of the volume of text in the parallel now rests on YHWH's punishing characteristics. Third, the overall impact of the rehearsal of the credo here is that YHWH is a jealous, punishing God so that even the mercy that is given is only to those that "love me and keep my commands."

First, this parallel has not only altered the original order of attributes within the two poles of the credo, but it has also actually reversed the order of the two poles. The overall effect of this reversal is that YHWH's wrath is emphasized. The God who brings the punishment for idolatry brings it not only to the unrighteous, but also to their offspring. The wrath of YHWH is taken up and emphasized to prohibit/scare/warn the ancient Israelites from false worship, either of YHWH or the other gods. In the original, the emphasis lies on YHWH's forgiveness and compassion, which is tempered by the secondary pole that announces his wrathfulness. In this parallel, YHWH's punishment and wrath is tempered by forgiveness and compassion.

Second, this parallel also shifts the emphasis onto YHWH's wrath by adding extra literary volume to that pole. The amount of literary volume given to YHWH's punishing is more than three times that given to merciful attributes (in Hebrew, 10 words to 3 words). In the original, the word count is even with both poles having 15 words. This heavy redaction of the merciful aspects of YHWH's character furthers the emphasis on the harsh judgment that comes on those that worship idols or images.

Third, both poles are modified by additional phrases. The punishment given will be placed upon "those who hate me," but the mercy of YHWH will be extended to "those who love me and keep my commands." These additions clarify the ambiguity of the earlier version of the credo which a later redactor did not believe adequately delineated why some were the objects of wrath and some were extended mercy. Sarna translates לשׂנאי as "those who reject me" and follows rabbinic authors who believed that the redactor who inserted this phrase "seized upon the ambiguity [of the original credo] to soften the apparent harshness" by showing that the vertical retribution was only administered to those of the later generations who "perpetuated the evils of their parents."[45] There are several examples of this type of redaction by Dtr. Deut 7:7–11 contains close thematic and linguistic parallels proclaiming that YHWH maintains covenant faithfulness to those loving God and keeping God's commands, while punishing those who hate him. Deut 24:16 also states that God's punishment is not without reason, as fathers and sons will only be put to death for their own sins. The same phrases also occur in the Deuteronomy version of the Decalogue (5:11).

Participation in the Larger Pericope

In the most narrow literary context, this parallel of the credo comes as a part of the Ten Commandments as added emphasis for the first two commandments. In the Decalogue, the first two commands deal with right worship of YHWH— worship of other Gods (I) and ancient Israel's aniconic nature (II). H.W. Obbink has argued that the images refer not to images of YHWH, but to images of other gods, mostly based upon the reasoning that YHWH could not be "jealous" of an image of himself.[46] Childs has refuted Obbink's hypothesis based on two major factors.[47] First, the justification of the command and the command were not originally linked, which does not help identify the original meaning of "image" as YHWH's jealously was not originally part of it.[48] YHWH's jealously cannot be used to determine the meaning of image, because it was not originally connected. Second, the "general picture of pre-monarchic Hebrew religion seems to confirm the judgment that images of Yahweh were forbidden, even though contraventions are recorded."[49] With these arguments in mind, it can be argued that I and II are more intimately

---

45. Sarna, *Exodus = [Shemot]*, 111.

46. Obbink, "Jahwebilder," 264–74.

47. Childs, *The Book of Exodus*, 404.

48. See also Zimmerli, "Das zweite Gebot," 234–48; and von Rad, *Old Testament Theology*, 1:212–19, who make similar arguments.

49. Childs, *The Book of Exodus*, 404. See also Mettinger, "The Veto on Images," 15–29.

linked than any of the other commands. In fact, rabbinic tradition treats I and II as a single unit.[50] Both deal with right worship. Right worship must intentionally focus on YHWH and not on images or idols.

The second commandment expressly forbids both idols (פֶּסֶל) and images (תְּמוּנָה). The separation of the two by *vav* in this version of the Decalogue was seemingly done to provide an antecedent for the "to them" (20:5a). In Deuteronomy 5, the literary connection between I and II is much closer so that the "to them" of Deut 5:9 refers to the "other gods" of I (Deut 5:7).[51] The basic meaning of the commandment is that no physical form of YHWH is to be constructed for cultic purposes. The insertion of the parallel after these two commandments heightens the intensity of their theological force.

The reason why the ancient Israelites must worship properly is because YHWH is a "jealous God" (אֵל קַנָּא). YHWH's jealousy is a common Deuteronomic theme. The next occurrence is in the "Ritual Decalogue" of Exodus 34. In 34:14, the text is again associated with a commandment not to worship other gods because not only is YHWH a jealous God, but his name is "Jealous." In Deut 4:24, YHWH's jealousy is again brought to the fore by a prohibition against idol worship. In this context, it is compared to a devouring fire. In Deut 6:15, the people are again warned not to worship other gods on account of YHWH's jealousy. In every instance that the epithet אֵל קַנָּא is used, it refers to YHWH's jealousy because of idol worship or worship of other gods.[52] Thus, its location after the two commands prohibiting idol worship and worship of other gods is not only natural, but even expected.

Sarna translates the epithet as an "impassioned God."[53] He begins by noting that the primary meaning of the root is "to become intensely red," and later came to denote strong emotions because of the tendency of the coloration of the face to change during times of extreme emotion. He rejects the usual translation of a "jealous God" because of its connotations

50. Sarna, *Exodus = [Shemot]*, 109.

51. Johnstone, *Exodus*, 90.

52. There are six other occurrences of קַנָּא which are closely associated with YHWH. Deuteronomy 32 gives an account of how the people stirred God's jealousy by worshipping other gods and idols (32:16, 21). 1 Kings 14 tells of how the people of Judah brought out YHWH's jealousy by their idolatry (14:22). The remaining four are eschatological visions of God's future passion for Zion or Israel (Ezek 39:25; Joel 2:18; Zech 1:14; 8:2).

53 Sarna, *Exodus = [Shemot]*, 110.

of the marriage metaphor. Using the marriage metaphor, God's reaction to ancient Israel's unfaithfulness is jealousy. Sarna combats this interpretation by noting that the form קַנָּא is only used to describe God and not humans. This distinction shows that the biblical writers imagined a qualitatively different kind of emotion for God that was not present in the human psyche. It shows that "God cannot be indifferent to His creatures" and it underscores "the vigorous, intensive, and punitive nature of the divine response to apostasy and to modes of worship unacceptable to Himself."[54] While Sarna's point is well taken, the metaphor has limits, as all do. Nevertheless, this marriage metaphor may be the best at describing how the ancient Israelites understood their relationship to God. The association of the parallel with YHWH's jealousy intensifies the emphasis on the strong covenantal relationship between ancient Israel and their God.

Jealousy is an emotion that becomes most apparent when one person has acted in a negative way in a relationship. Cassuto remarks that YHWH's jealousy for the nation does not carry positive implications. Cassuto imagines YHWH saying that if ancient Israel acts "toward Me [YHWH] like a faithless wife, a spirit of jealousy will pass over Me, and you will suffer severe punishment for breaking My covenant."[55]

On the larger literary scale, this parallel of the credo is located during the initial giving of the covenant stipulations required by the Sinai Covenant. Childs has rightly delineated the central place of the Decalogue within the overall structure of Exodus.[56] The prologue (20:2),

---

54. Sarna, *Exodus*, 110. Peels ("קנא," 937–40) also rejects the use of the marriage metaphor and instead opts for the lord/vassal metaphor because of the object of the wrath; a scorned husband fixates anger on the other man, not on the unfaithful wife ("קנא" in Van Gemeren, *The New International Dictionary of Old Testament Theology & Exegesis* 3:937–40). I find this argument to be unconvincing—unfaithfulness incites anger at both the offending spouse and the person with whom the offense occurred. On the other hand, E. Rueter uses the law codes of Num 5:11–31, which deal with jealousy between a husband and wife that is suspected to be unfaithful, to illustrate the meaning of the term ("קנא qn’" in *Theological Dictionary of the Old Testament*, 13:49). G. Sauer emphasizes the exclusivity and uniqueness of the relationship that YHWH demands in that other ancient Near Eastern religions never speak of a god being jealous for a worshiper ("קִנְאָה qin’a fervor" in *Theological Lexicon of the Old Testament*, 3:1146).

55. Cassuto, *A Commentary on the Book of Exodus*, 242–43.

56. Childs, *Introduction to the Old Testament*, 174.

which announces God's deliverance of the people out of slavery, summarizes the first 18 chapters of Exodus. The Decalogue also points forward as it encapsulates all of the commands to come. Childs notes, "There is a comprehensiveness to the commandments which sets the Decalogue apart from other series."[57] In this scheme, the Ten Commandments occupy a central place in the overall literary structure of Exodus. Further, the parallel's location in a preeminent place within a preeminent text highlights its importance.

The manipulation of the parallel in this instance places most of the covenant responsibility onto ancient Israel. YHWH's grace and wrath are given respectively to those that love or hate the commandments. YHWH's merciful attributes recorded in 34:6–7 were severely truncated and deemphasized in favor of a picture of a wrathful God. This placement enunciates the nation's responsibility in keeping the covenant. The full burden of covenant faithfulness is placed upon the people even as are the harsh consequences of not keeping the covenant.

From our study of the parallel of Exod 34:6–7 placed in the Decalogue of Exodus 20, we can make four summary affirmations.

1. The manipulation of the credo was performed in such a way to emphasize God's wrath and ancient Israel's responsibility in keeping the covenant.

2. The addition of the phrase "jealous God" greatly intensified the covenantal character of the credo.

3. The controlling factors of "those who hate" and "those who love" were added to show that YHWH's mercy or wrath was not arbitrary, but directed toward those who deserved it.

4. The parallel's climactic position in the Exodus narrative highlights its importance in the covenantal relationship between YHWH and ancient Israel.

EXODUS 34

Diachronic Issues

Because many of the diachronic issues associated with the text of Exod 34:6–7 were discussed in chapter 1, this section will be brief, focusing

57. Ibid., 174.

only on a short summary of the major diachronic issues present in Exodus 32–34. Any such discussion must begin with Wellhausen's comparison of the material with the pericope of chapters 19–24 both of which contain Decalogues— an ethical Decalogue in Exodus 20 composed by E and a ritual Decalogue in Exodus 34 composed by J.[58] Unfortunately, scholars have reached no consensus on the actual source reconstruction of the pericope.[59] Form critics have had no more success at reaching a consensus than source critics. For example, von Rad and Mendenhall come to radically different conclusions based on form-critical methodology. Mendenhall believes that the Sinai materials are based on ancient Hittite treaties and are very old, while von Rad argues that the Sinai tradition was one of the last things added to the core formulation of ancient Israel's history that was built upon the *kleine credo*.[60] The results of redaction critics have also been inconclusive. Childs believes that a JE redactor produced a text very similar to its final form, although a Deuteronomic redactor put the final touches on the text.[61] Conversely, R.W.L. Moberly, who has done the most extensive analysis of Exodus 32–34, argues that the text shows no signs of a Deuteronomic redactor.[62] The overall results of diachronic analysis are far from conclusive and without any real consensus.

Any strong diachronic affirmations should be avoided. The most generally agreed upon fact is that Exodus 32–34 is mostly a product of JE. In a summary statement, Childs calls the JE redactor's work almost author-like because of the extent of his work.[63] After this redaction, any later emendations by D are difficult to find as even the things labeled as D could be proto-Deuteronomic. Most commentators believe that the credo was part of Exodus 32–34 by sometime late in the monarchy. In this context, the passage would have shown that the disobedient nation's only hope for survival rested in the capricious mercy of YHWH.

---

58. Wellhausen, *Die Composition des Hexateuchs*, 332–36.

59. For a helpful summary of six different reconstructions of the conclusions of source critics, see Pigott, "God of Compassion and Mercy," 233–37 (appendix A). Pigott concludes that, "The result is that while most interpreters agree that these chapters are composed primarily of J and E, the variations are endless and often quite complex" (14).

60. Mendenhall, "Covenant Forms in Israelite Tradition," 50–76; and von Rad, "The Form-Critical Problem of the Hexateuch," 20–26.

61. Childs, *The Book of Exodus*, 610.

62. Moberly, *At the Mountain of God*, 185–86.

63. Childs, *The Book of Exodus*, 610.

During the late monarchy, this original narrative context of the credo would have given those who were watching the monarchy crumble an expectation that renewal could be achieved. As YHWH forgave the nation for its worship of the Golden Calf, so could the people of the later time be forgiven. The narrative then, stood as a stark reminder that YHWH in no way allows worship of idols, but their relationship can be quickly restored.

Participation in Exodus 34:6–7

This step in the methodology will be skipped as this passage is Exod 34:6–7.

Participation in the Larger Pericope

In Exodus 32–34, the credo functions as both the climax and unifying feature of the narrative. As the climax, it is the fruition of God's forgiveness of the disobedient people. The pericope begins with the people's dramatic apostasy while Moses was actually still receiving the laws of the covenant. YHWH informs Moses of the apostasy and Moses dramatically intercedes for the people, calling upon God not to kill all of them. Moses then summons all of the faithful Levites to seek vengeance. Eventually, 3000 of the disobedient people are killed. In chapter 33, Moses again intercedes for the people and amazingly asks to see God face to face. YHWH partially grants Moses' request of theophany allowing Moses to see God's back. The climax of the pericope comes as YHWH fully agrees to be merciful to the people during the theophany and giving of the credo. The short narrative ends with the regiving of the covenant stipulations and a "ritual Decalogue" parallel to chapter 20's "ethical Decalogue."

Synchronically, this text completely reverses the emphasis on the harsh, judging God of Exodus 20:5. This second appearance of the credo changes the whole tenor of the relationship between YHWH and ancient Israel. This new version stresses God's unconditional mercy to be heaped on the nation. Fretheim notes, "The doubling of the emphasis upon God's steadfast love and the omission of the conditional elements stress the unconditionality of the divine love to Israel."[64] The loss of the conditional elements of "those who love me and keep my commands"

64. Fretheim, *Exodus*, 302.

and "those who hate me" along with the doubling of the positive characterization of YHWH's mercy show that God's compassion will outweigh the heinous sin of the people. In this instance, YHWH's mercy is unconditional. Janzen postulates that the importance of the credo at this literary and theological time lies in the fact that "in the face of Israel's most grievous covenant betrayal, El Shaddai . . . becomes manifest as El Raḥum we-Ḥanun, 'God compassionate and gracious.' This is to suggest that El Raḥum we-Ḥanun not only exegetes the divine name Yahweh but also does so in terms of El Shaddai."[65] Janzen's point is that this text, for the first time, shows a different side of the God of the fathers. The God of the fathers in 3:15 is now shown as the gracious and compassionate one. Furthermore, the giving of the credo is the fulfillment of the promise given to Moses in 33:18–23. The author emphasized this connection by the use of the key word "pass by" and "proclaim the name."[66]

This occurrence of the parallel carries four significant connections with the first canonical appearance in Exodus 20. First, the irony of YHWH forgiving the people's idolatry with a proclamation about the divine nature that has strong connections to the second commandment should not be quickly overlooked. The text receives extra force in the narrative as the harsh, wrathful emphasis of the previous parallel is inverted toward YHWH's mercy. Second, each parallel is closely connected to covenant stipulations.[67] In Exodus 20, the parallel begins the Decalogue which is part of the initial giving of the covenant to the people. In Exodus

---

65. Janzen, *Exodus*, 254.

66. Childs, *The Book of Exodus*, 612.

67. There has been significant discussion about the two different Decalogues present in Exodus 20 and Exodus 34. Samuel R. Driver states "[I]t has been supposed that these verses, though now expanded by the compiler, consisted originally of ten commands forming a 'ritual decalogue' (as opposed to the 'moral Decalogue' of ch. 20)" [*Introduction to the Literature of the Old Testament*, 39]. It seems that Driver's distinction is misplaced for two reasons. First, the distinction between things cultic/ritual and things moral is certainly modern and without place in the ancient world. Second, numbering the commandments is difficult and finding ten takes significant interpretive work. For others who oppose this distinction between ritual and moral see Johnstone, *Exodus*, 80–81 and Childs, *The Book of Exodus*, 396. In my opinion, the phrase "Ten Commands" (34:28) refers back to the commands of Exodus 20, in spite of the fact that this instance is the first time that the Decalogue is called the "Ten Commands." Synchronically speaking, this option is the most logical, as God gives the commands again and reestablishes the covenant.

34, several commands follow the theophany (34:17–26) as does a reference back to the original Decalogue (34:28).

Third, each parallel is marked by a connection to the "jealous God." Exodus 34:14 states, "Do not worship any other god, because YHWH, whose name is 'Jealous,' is a jealous God." The covenant intensifies as not only is YHWH a jealous God, but his very name is "Jealous." Also as noted the above, the term has strong covenantal overtones. The covenant intensifies in this instance, as YHWH is now not only pro-ancient Israel, but is actively against the other nations. Both immediately before and immediately after the affirmation that YHWH is a jealous God, the text announces that this jealous God will drive out the other nations.[68] The people must not make treaties with them, marry their daughters or attend their cultic services, but completely destroy their cultic sites. YHWH's strong affinity toward the ancient Israelites also carries with it a rejection of the other nations. Fourth, both passages also carry theophanic language.[69] Exodus 34:5 states that YHWH "came down in a cloud" which combines elements of God's descent in 19:16,18. In both cases, neither humans nor animals are allowed on the sacred mountain (19:12; 34:3). The overall result of these four major similarities is that the narrator intentionally recalls the first giving of the covenant and contrasts it with this reestablishment of the relationship. The newly established covenant places more emphasis on YHWH's forgiveness and mercy in order to maintain the covenant.

The following summary affirmations highlight the importance of the confession in Exodus 34:

1. This appearance of the parallel is the fullest manifestation of the credo.
2. The fact that the credo is delivered in a theophany from YHWH's own mouth highlights its importance.
3. The parallel is again connected with YHWH's jealousy emphasizing the covenantal implications of the text.

---

68. While this proclamation is not the first time in Exodus that YHWH has declared that he will drive out the other nations (cf. Exod 23:28; 32:2), it is the first time that YHWH's jealousy is so closely associated with the driving out of the other nations.

69. Childs, *The Book of Exodus*, 611.

4. The narrative context surrounding the credo establishes the fact that the survival of the covenantal relationship is heavily dependent upon God's grace and mercy.

NUMBERS 14

The parallel of Exod 34:6–7 found in Numbers 14 is the most complete rehearsal of the credo found in the Hebrew Bible. In fact, it is almost a verbatim comparison. It is also found in a very similar narrative to Exodus 32–34. In both cases, the covenant is endangered because of the people's sin, either idolatry or rebellion. Per the custom, the diachronic factors will first be considered, followed by the parallel's participation in Exod 34:6–7 and finally how this parallel fits into the surrounding narrative.

Diachronic Issues

The majority consensus is that the final form of this parallel is the work of P.[70] Most believe that an earlier version of this story was significantly reworked by the P editor. Certainly, the marks of P are strong throughout this narrative.[71] The cultic community is very organized, the role of Joshua is emphasized and a theophany is associated with the tent of meeting. Martin Noth represents the standard viewpoint. He believes that two easily recognizable strata are present—J and P.[72] He follows

70. Coats offers a source critical analysis which sees a basic J narrative that is reworked by P [*Rebellion in the Wilderness*, 137–39]; Gray sees a basic JE source with later P editing (*Critical and Exegetical Commentary on Numbers*, 128–33). William H. Bellinger Jr. believes the final form to be a result of a P editor operating during the exile [*Leviticus and Numbers*, 14]; Katherine Doob Sakenfeld also opts for an exilic P (*Journeying with God*, 3); Dennis T. Olson opts for a P editor shortly after the end of the exile [*Numbers*, 3]. Sean McEvenue sees a J source with a final P redaction, but also some post-P glosses present (e.g., 14:34) ["A Source Critical Problem in Num.14,26–38," 454–56]; See also Boorer, *The Promise of the Land as Oath*, 331; n.b. Boorer's extensive survey of source critical history. John van Seters also marks the final editor as P, but dates that editor circa 400 ("The Pentateuch," 44–45). I believe that Van Seters' P is too late based on the thematic similarities between the exilic/early post-exilic community and the text (listed below).

71. See Blenkinsopp for a summary of these marks of P's redaction (*The Pentateuch*, 163–64).

72. Noth, *Numbers: A Commentary* 101–2. Interestingly, Noth believes that this story is the first indication of any conquest theme (101).

this premise with his usual traditio-critical explanation that the two are structured around their cultic heroes; J emphasized the role of Caleb and P's later additions preferred Joshua. Later, Ludwig Schmidt argued from source-critical grounds that the two easily deciphered sources of Numbers 13–14, along with the parallel spy story of Deut 1:19–46 show that Wellhausen's Documentary Hypothesis is still the most viable as opposed to the many newer hypotheses about Pentateuchal origins that do not hold to the merging of whole separate histories of ancient Israel.[73] In either case, the vast majority of scholars argue for two (usually) easily delineated narratives in the text, an early J or JE source, which is later emended by a late exilic or early post-exilic P.

In conclusion, it is easy to imagine how the exilic community for which P was writing could have identified with the community of Numbers 13–14. Joseph Blenkinsopp lists three major thematic parallels between the exilic community and the literary community.[74] Both communities would have been inundated with fears and hopes about entry or reentry into the land— "We seemed like grasshoppers in our own eyes, and we looked the same to them" (Num 13:33). Second, each community would have had to deal with conflicting reports about the economic prospects of the land as the community dealt with the pros and cons of taking the land—"[The Land] does flow with milk and honey . . . But the people who live there are powerful and the cities are fortified and very large." (Num 13:27b–28). Third, the community of Numbers 13–14 was scared away by the larger than life natives living who would make taking the land very difficult—"We saw the Nephillim there" (Num 13:33).

The parallel of the credo in this text would have reminded the exiled community that their only hope rested in the mercy of YHWH. The faithfulness of Joshua, Caleb and Moses would become exemplars for the disenfranchised exilic people. Numbers 13–14 proclaims that only a faith which understands that YHWH's mercy and subsequent support were the only hope for retaking the land is acceptable. William H. Bellinger notes, "The hope that the chapter proclaims is one born of divine judgment, surely a perspective understood by people in exile."[75] The resonance of this text with the late exilic/early post-exilic community is clear.

73. Schmidt, "Die Kundschaftererzählung in Num 13–14 und Dtn 1,19–46," 40–58.

74. Blenkinsopp, *The Pentateuch*, 164.

75. Bellinger, *Leviticus and Numbers*, 232.

The resounding message would have been full of hope and promise. The community only need trust in YHWH and his propensity toward the forgiveness of their sin.

Participation in Exodus 34:6–7

This parallel of the credo is the most complete rehearsal found in the Hebrew Bible. Six aspects of the original credo were emended from this version:

1. YHWH
2. Compassionate and gracious God
3. and faithfulness
4. Extending loving kindness to the thousandth generation
5. and sin
6. on the children's children.

The first emendation may simply be explained as a reduction of the double naming of YHWH of the original.[76] The second emendation comes as the most surprising and difficult to explain. YHWH's characteristics of רחום and חנון would have fit very naturally within the context in which Moses was reminding YHWH of his previous forgiveness of the rebellious nation. Milgrom postulates that this omission had to do with the basic nature of Moses' plea—he did not seek complete cancellation of the punishment, but simply its postponement.[77] Pigott opts for a similar reading as she proposes that this omission places emphasis on YHWH's slowness to anger.[78] Indeed, the narrative of Numbers 14 supports the assertions of Pigott and Milgrom as YHWH does not completely dismiss the punishment, but simply postpones it. The rebellious people would not be wiped out instantaneously in the desert, but now over a whole generation. The third emendation (faithfulness) may be explained by its close connection with "truth" and "justice" (e.g., Exod 18:21; Neh 7:2; Ps 85:11). Moses did not want the ancient Israelites to be dealt with "justly," but rather mercifully. The people deserved death, but he requested grace.

---

76. The LXX also omits the second יהוה.

77. Milgrom, *Numbers* במדבר, 111.

78. Pigott, "God of Compassion and Mercy," 129–30.

The fourth emendation (extending loving kindness to the thousandth generation) is a more difficult revision to understand. Milgrom follows the same logic that he uses for the loss of God's compassion and grace, again stating that Moses is not seeking cancellation but postponement.[79] Contrarily, it would seem most natural for Moses to provoke the extension of God's mercy to the innumerable generations. The most likely reason for its omission is again the connection to the narrative. The rebellious generation will die in the desert and their children will be shepherds for forty years (Num 14:31–33). Moses' plea for mercy to the thousandth generation would have been inappropriate within the context of this narrative. The fifth emendation omits YHWH's taking away of חטאה. This omission highlights the other two nouns of this participial string—iniquity and transgression. Milgrom notes that חטאה may have been omitted because it refers to inadvertent sin and the people's rebellion was open and deliberate (cf. Lev 4:2).[80] Pigott holds that the omission puts the emphasis squarely upon פשע, the second noun of the participial string, which she translates as "rebellion."[81] She notes, "This word for sin is particularly applicable to the context of Numbers since the primary sin of the people is their rebellion and lack of trust."[82] The sixth and final emendation (on the children's children) produces no significant alteration in the meaning of the credo as the force of punishment to the "third and fourth generations" is still present.

Despite these six emendations, this version of the credo is remarkably similar to the original. First, each rehearses God's merciful characteristics. While the rehearsal of God's mercy is significantly truncated, the fact that it remains in the first position is significant. Three aspects of the positive portrayal of YHWH are given. YHWH's slowness to anger and great loving kindness would have been extremely important to Moses as he pleaded for God's mercy to the people. At this time in the narrative, the only hope for the people rested in God's ability to forgive their iniquity and transgression. The limitations on YHWH's loving kindness of Exodus 20 which were based upon commandment keeping and loving YHWH are again absent as the narrative context shows that the people are certainly undeserving of God's postponement of wrath.

79. Milgrom, *Numbers*, 111.
80. Ibid.
81. Pigott, "God of Compassion and Mercy," 130.
82. Ibid.

Surprisingly, the aspects of God's wrath were emended in only a minor way and with no significant theological departure from the original. Again, the rehearsal fits the narrative context as YHWH's mercy does not override the divine wrath; it postpones it. In Num 14:20–25, the Lord agrees to forgive them, "Even as [Moses] asked." Yet, none of the disobedient generation will get to see the Promised Land. By keeping the inherent theological tension of the credo, this parallel functions to remind the reader that YHWH's mercy is not freely given nor is the divine wrath easily withheld from those who have broken covenant.

Participation in the Larger Pericope

The narrative of Numbers 13–14 comes at a climactic point in the overall narrative of Numbers. Dennis Olson has noted that the rebellion of these chapters is preceded by three increasingly serious uprisings.[83] The first rebellion involved some murmurings on the outskirts of the camp (11:1–3); YHWH responds by reigning fire down upon the offenders. The second rebellion comes as the whole crowd of ancient Israelites complains about the lack of variety in their diet (11:4–35); YHWH initially grants them meat in the form of innumerable quail to eat, but eventually strikes them with a great plague (11:33). The third rebellion centers on Miriam and Aaron's rejection of Moses' leadership because of his Egyptian wife (12:1–16); YHWH's punishment is turning Miriam's skin white with leprosy, but he heals her soon after (12:9–17). Olson has given special attention to the fact that in each of the rebellions, the involvement of the people escalates.[84] The rebellion moves from the outskirts of the camp, to the whole crowd, to even infiltrating the leaders. Olson notes, "In the spy story, both the leaders in the form of the spies (13:2) and all the people (14:1–2) are involved and implicated."[85] The intensity of the rebellion of Numbers 13–14 increases as the people reject their leaders, reject YHWH and threaten to return to Egypt.[86] What Coats calls the "murmuring tradition" wishes to "reverse the Exodus" by a "rejection of this deity and a move to elect a new leader to take the people back to

---

83. Olson, *Numbers*, 81.

84. Ibid.

85. Ibid.

86. Coats, *Rebellion in the Wilderness*, 146.

Egypt."[87] The rebellion of the spy story is complete and unprecedented in Numbers for severity.

In addition to its relation to the previous three rebellions, the spy narrative stands as a central piece of the overall narrative of the book. Olson states, "More than any other story in Numbers, the spy narrative in chapters 13–14 lays the foundation for the unifying structure in the theme of the book."[88] Bellinger simply calls the chapters, "A watershed that determines the course of a generation in Israel."[89] Ashley also takes these chapters to be central based upon verbal connections with the two central censuses of the book.[90] These chapters are central for two reasons. First, the narrative comes as the people are ready to enter the land. The reader has been anticipating entry into the land since God's promise to Abraham in Genesis 12 and again reemphasized with the Exodus from Egypt. The book of Numbers heightens this anticipation with the census of Numbers 1 to prepare for entry. Second, the narrative also explains the reasons for the wilderness wanderings of the remainder of the book. It is within this climactic position that the third appearance of the credo comes in the Pentateuch.

The story has many parallels to the Golden Calf narrative of Exodus 32–34 and the two will be compared in detail here. In each instance, the rebellion and sinfulness of the people encompass the whole community. In the Golden Calf narrative, all of the people worship the calf manufactured by Aaron even as all of the people rebelled against the leadership of Moses by following the unfaithful spies. In this spy narrative, the narrator goes to lengths to show that only Joshua and Caleb did not rebel (14:6, 30, 38). Katherine Doob Sakenfeld makes special note of the seriousness of נאץ "to despise."[91] She suggests that the rebellion is not simply based upon their disbelief about entry into the land, but that it is also a complete rejection of the entire covenant with YHWH. "The goal of God's relationship with the people from the moment of their

87. Ibid.

88. Olson, *Numbers*, 75.

89. Bellinger, *Leviticus, Numbers*, 228.

90. Ashley, *The Book of Numbers*, 230. In Numbers 1, those numbered are those "twenty years and up" while in 14:29, those same ones "twenty years and up" are the ones punished. In 26:64–65 the text reminds the reader that none of the original ones counted are counted in the second census.

91. Sakenfeld, *Journeying with God*, 89.

departure from Egypt has been to bring them to the land promised to their ancestors (Gen. 12:7). To refuse to enter the land is to reject the goal of the relationship."[92] This far reaching sin must be punished and punished severely.

The effect of this rejection can be seen in YHWH's response. God gives a double exclamation, (עַד־אָנָה) "How long . . ." in 14:11.[93] The phrase is often found in laments and complaints that hold that the deity has broken the covenant.[94] The unbelievable disbelief of the people caused God deep and glaring pain.

Second, in each narrative God wants to wipe out the people and begin again with Moses. In Exod 32:10 and Num 14:12, God's initial reaction is harsh punishment upon the people and then a reestablishment of a covenant people under Moses. These two threats are the only two times in the Pentateuch in which YHWH threatens to wipe out the people completely. This initial judgment which would have resulted in the complete annihilation of the people stands as the harshest of the punishments given for any of the rebellious acts of the people. In each of the previous three, the punishment matched the rebellion—those murmuring on the fringes of the camp were struck with a plague, the people ate meat until they were inundated with it after complaining of their diet consisting only of manna, and finally Miriam's skin turned white after her rejection of Moses' wife of Egyptian heritage. This punishment shows that the people's rejection of YHWH will result in YHWH's rejection of them.

Won W. Lee offers three other connections of the Exodus tradition to the threat to punish after the Golden Calf narrative.[95] First, YHWH intends to strike the people with a pestilence. The last time that a plague was used as a punishment was against Pharaoh. Second, the destruction of the people would be a direct reversal of the people acting as God's inheritance (Exod 34:9). Third, God offers to begin again with Moses which is an extension of the initial offer given (Exod 32:10). The reversal

---

92. Ibid.

93. For a rhetorical analysis of these two exclamations, see Newing, "The Rhetoric of Altercation in Numbers 14," 211–28, esp. 213. Olson holds that these texts show YHWH to be "angry and despairing" (*Numbers*, 80).

94. Cf. Ps 13:2–3; Hab 1:2.

95. Lee, *Punishment and Forgiveness*, 226.

of the plagues of the Exodus and God's disinheritance of the people show the severity of the punishment intended.

Third, Moses understands the severity of the punishment and immediately offers intercession on behalf of the people just as in Exod 32:11. In the spy narrative, Moses' petition has two parts. The first is a repetition and direct parallel of Exod 32:12—Moses makes a direct appeal to YHWH's pride as he summons the possibility of an unfavorable report given to the Egyptians which would make ancient Israel's deity seem powerless to bring the people into the land. Moses increases the intensity of the petition given in Exodus 32 by adding that the Egyptians will be so enamored with the report of YHWH's futility, that they will certainly tell the other nations. These other nations will proclaim, "YHWH was not able." The nations will not hear the whole story; they will believe that YHWH simply slaughtered the people in the desert because of an inability to defeat either Pharaoh or the deities of the native inhabitants of the land. Moses' first petition clearly puts the reputation of YHWH's power at stake as opposed to YHWH's grace.

Interestingly, Moses' initial petition also brings the other nations into play. The petition as given in Exodus 32 did not mention the taunts of the other nations; it simply states that the report of YHWH's actions will return to the Egyptians. Olson believes that this statement shows that, "God is interested in being known by other nations besides Israel."[96] This exclamation foreshadows later uses of the credo to be discussed in chapters 3 and 4 of this study. In the Twelve, YHWH's interaction with the other nations is highlighted by the credo. In the Psalter, the reign of YHWH over the whole earth is enunciated even more clearly by psalms that contain the credo. This use of the credo foreshadows a future canonical thematic movement toward YHWH as king over the nations and over the whole earth.

Moses' second petition is a return to YHWH's own speech. Ashley notes that Moses' second petition differs from the first in that it was "based not on the nations' perceptions of Yahweh's reality, but on the reality of Israel's perception of Yahweh, viz., his mercy, covenant loyalty, and forgiveness."[97] Moses' second petition actually uses God's own words

96. Olson, *Numbers*, 82.

97. Ashley, *Numbers*, 257. See Olson, *Numbers*, who believes there to be three separate petitions, by dividing the giving of the credo (14:18) and an appeal to YHWH's

to remind the Deity that covenant fidelity is the nation's only hope to save the nation. Sakenfeld holds that the forgiveness of the people rests completely in YHWH and God's "surprising act of sheer grace."[98] Olson, more appropriately, argues that Moses' reminder of YHWH's own speech is a reminder that, "God has an obligation to make good on promises made in the past."[99] As noted above, the credo underwent significant modifications. Elements of mercy and grace were significantly modified specifically for this context. The credo's manifestation here reminds YHWH of the divine responsibility and ability to forgive while at the same time leaving theological room for the punishment of the people.

The petitions end with Moses' general request for pardon for the people in which he again stresses the divine "loving kindness" and YHWH's past covenantal mercy on the people. Milgrom believes that the repetition of the terms "iniquity," "loving kindness" and "forgiveness" in Moses' general petition are intended to recall all of YHWH's merciful handling of the disobedient nation from the time of Exodus until even now.[100] Lee takes the phrases and the passage to be designed to recall not only the Exodus, but even the promise to Abraham.[101] Lee bases this claim on the fact that YHWH's remembrance of the slaves was because of God's covenant with Abraham to give him the Land.

In slight contrast to the three major parallels with the Golden Calf narrative, the two stories also contain some slight differences. First, God's forgiveness of the people is not concluded with a reestablishment/reaffirmation of the covenant as in Exodus 34. After God forgives the people in Exodus 34, the covenant and new stipulations are given to the people. No such renewal comes in Numbers 14. Second, judgment upon the people is only postponed, not pardoned. In the Golden Calf narrative, God fully intends to wipe out all of the people, but instead opts for a pardon of the people. In the spy narrative, God again fully intends to wipe out all of the people. In this narrative, however, God does not fully pardon the judgment, but simply postpones it—the unrighteous

past mercy (14:19) as two separate units (83). I believe that this division may see an improper distinction between these two. Moses' appeal to the credo is also an appeal to past mercy.

98. Sakenfeld, *Journeying with God*, 91.

99. Olson, *Numbers*, 82.

100. Milgrom, *Numbers*, 112.

101. Lee, *Punishment and Forgiveness*, 227.

generation will die before they are able to enter the land.[102] While the credo is central in both texts, the result is slightly different. Third, this use of the parallel is the only one of four appearances in the Torah not to be explicitly connected to idol worship. While this narrative certainly involved disobedience, it was not connected to idolatry.

There are five summary affirmations from our study of Numbers 14:

1. The credo maintained the basic shape of its original form with emphasis on YHWH's grace.

2. The credo again comes at a point in which the covenant relationship between YHWH and ancient Israel is endangered.

3. This appearance of the credo introduces the first interaction between YHWH and the other nations.

4. This appearance of the credo gives a dramatic example of the tension proclaimed as YHWH forgives by postponing the judgment upon the disobedient generation.

5. This appearance of the credo is the only one of the four Pentateuchal parallels to be connected with neither idolatry nor YHWH's jealousy.

DEUTERONOMY 5

The fourth and final parallel of the credo occurs in the second giving of the Decalogue in Deuteronomy 5. As the people are moving into the land, the book of Deuteronomy records a dramatic renewal of the covenant on the plains of Moab. As Moses bids the people farewell, he also admonishes them to continue keeping the covenant. The parallel comes in the Decalogue which is given at the beginning of the covenant renewal ceremony.

---

102. See Milgrom, *Numbers*, who argues that the people are not pardoned in Exodus 34, but their judgment is simply postponed (112). Milgrom bases his argument on the work of George Coats who believes that there are no instances of forgiveness in the "murmuring scenes" which begin in Exod 14:11 (*Rebellion in the Wilderness*, 148–50); see also Knierem and Coats, *Numbers*, 188. For this reason, Milgrom translates סלח as "reconciliation" rather than "forgiveness." While Milgrom's distinction may be technically right, there does some to be a significant practical difference between YHWH's reaction after the two rebellions.

Diachronic Issues

Many of the diachronic issues related to the Decalogue were covered in our discussion of Exodus 20. As noted there, the consensus of the majority is that the Decalogue of Deuteronomy 5 is a product of the exilic Deuteronomist. The major difference between the two commands comes in IV. The Sabbath command's remembrance of the Exodus in Deuteronomy would have provided a strong memory for the broken nation. Brueggemann notes, "The Sabbath is to be an occasion of *distinctive memory* of the Exodus. This memory of emancipation guards against the amnesia of the world of production that seeks to talk Israel out of its identity by vetoing its past."[103] This D version of the Decalogue would have sought to capture the imagination of the exiled nation. The use of the credo within this time would have again reminded the people that YHWH's covenantal grace was available, but only to those who kept the commands. The relationship with YHWH could be rejuvenated, but only with concrete acts of obedience. The reentry into the land would in no way be given without some active participation and covenant keeping by the people. The emphasis on YHWH's wrath would have prompted the people to obey the covenant stipulations.

Participation in Exodus 34:6–7

The participation in Exodus 34:6–7 of this passage is the same as the parallel of the credo from Exodus 20.

Participation in the Larger Narrative

Again, the immediate context of the parallel is in the second command prohibiting the worship of idols. The wording of the prohibition is different than in the Exodus version of the Decalogue. The Deuteronomy version (פסל כל־תמונה) of the passage does not include a *vav* between פסל and כל־תמונה as does the Exodus version. Thus, Deut 5:8 prohibits the worship of "an image of any shape" and Exod 20:4 prohibits the worship of "an image or any shape." The importance of this change is that now, the only available antecedent of "them" (להם) of 5:9 is the gods of I. This change links the first two commands more tightly than in

---

103. Brueggemann, *Deuteronomy*, 73.

Exodus.[104] The two prohibitions as they now stand command the people not to worship other gods or any images of YHWH.

As with the Decalogue of Exodus 20, the context for these two prohibitions is YHWH's jealousy. Patrick Miller sees a "double force" in this use of the epithet of a "jealous God."[105] As the people made themselves ready to enter the land, they would have seen these two implications of the affirmation of YHWH's jealousy. God required full and exclusive worship from the covenant people. In addition, the people would have also been aware of YHWH's commitment only to the ancient Israelites to love and care for them. Miller postulates that, "The jealousy of God, therefore, is that dimension within the divine encounter with the Lord's people that brooks no other final loyalty and ensures no other recipient of such unbounding love and grace. It is God's way of saying, I will have nothing less than your full devotion, and you will have nothing less than all my love."[106] The construction of an idol would be a weak attempt by the ancient Israelites to connive the presence of YHWH in their midst. The jealousy of YHWH prevented reliance on any sort of manufactured presence. The people are called to rely completely on YHWH's provision as they enter the land which demands an extreme act of faith by the covenant people.

In the larger narrative, the Decalogue again takes a preeminent place in the overall structure of Deuteronomy. The Ten Words are given first in the large section of laws that encompass the major portion of the book (5:1—26:19) which is framed by narrative on either side. Again, as in the Exodus 20 version, the credo is placed at the beginning of this very important group of laws. There has even been some discussion that highlights further the placement of the Decalogue within the overall structure of Deuteronomy. Thomas Mann sees the Decalogue as a defining literary paradigm for the laws of Deuteronomy 6–12.[107] This

---

104. Nelson, *Deuteronomy*, 80.

105. Miller, *Deuteronomy*, 76.

106. Ibid.

107. Mann, *Deuteronomy*, 49–90. Mann only finds a loose connection between the codes of the Ten Commandments and the later law codes. Many others see a more structured relationship between the two. Walton has argued that the Decalogue provides structure for the laws of chapters 6–26 ("Deuteronomy: An Exposition of the Spirit of the Law," 213–25). Braulik also finds a similar order between the order of the Decalogue and that of the ordinances of chapters 12–26 ("The Sequence of the Laws in Deuteronomy 12–26 and in the Decalogue," 313–35).

assumption is far from universal in the scholarly community. Ernest W. Nicholson believes that the codes exhibit no discernable structure.[108] Bernard Levinson argues that the covenant code receives its form from the fact that it is a revision/reinterpretation of the Covenant Code of Exodus 20:22–23:33.[109] Carmichael posits that the texts are arranged according to a wisdom pattern made of eight sections whereby the author first restates the laws of the Deuteronomic legal code, then references the early narratives of the Tetrateuch.[110] Thus there is no standard agreement on the order of the Deuteronomic laws or their relation to the Decalogue.

In any case, the Decalogue of Deuteronomy 5 comes first among the laws of Deuteronomy as it does in the covenant laws that begin in Exodus 20. This location testifies to the importance of these laws within the final form of the Pentateuch. The prologue to the laws (5:1–5) reminds the people of the previous covenant given to the people, but also emphasizes their stake in the relationship between the nation and YHWH. In fact, Moses proclaims that it was not with the forefathers and foremothers of the faith with whom the covenant was made, but with this contemporary generation (5:2–3). Moses emphasizes this fact with the piling on of temporal indicators in the Hebrew (אנחנו אלה פה היום כלנו חיים אתנו), which literally translated is "to us, we, these ones here today, all of the living ones." Miller notes, "The text uses seven words heaped upon one another to stress the contemporary claim of the covenant."[111] Furthermore, the text also identifies this generation as the generation of the theophany. In 5:4, Moses emphasizes the fact that this generation is the one to whom YHWH spoke to "from the middle of the fire." The text completely ignores the chronological and generational difference that has passed since the commands at Sinai. Interestingly, this occurrence of the credo is the only appearance in the Torah which does not literally come in a theophany. This text, however, places the people in the theophany of Exodus 19–20 along with the former generation.

---

108. Nicholson, *Deuteronomy and Tradition*, 33.

109. Levinson, *Deuteronomy and the Hermeneutics of Legal Innovation*, 3–22. See also his review of Carmichael's work, "Calum M. Carmichael's Approach to the Laws of Deuteronomy," 227–57.

110. Carmichael, *Laws of Deuteronomy*, 69–70, 94–95.

111. Miller, *Deuteronomy*, 67.

This discussion of the appearance of the credo within Deuteronomy 5 gives us four concluding reflections:

1. The parallel of the credo is again attached to the second commandment of the Decalogue and carries many of the same features.

2. The Decalogue and the credo appear in an important position in the overall structure of Deuteronomy as the first of all the covenant stipulations given.

3. The credo emphasizes God's wrath as motivation for keeping the covenant commands.

4. The younger generation is closely associated with the Sinai generation showing their burden to keep the covenantal jealousy of YHWH.

CONCLUSIONS

From the above examination of the role of the credo within the Torah, several summary affirmations can be made. First, the use of the credo throughout the history of ancient Israel indicates that the passage represented a core theological statement for the nation. The discussion above shows that the text occurs in a JE text (Exodus 34), a D text (Deuteronomy 5) and two P texts (Exodus 20 and Numbers 14). While it is certainly possible and maybe even probable that the texts represent earlier traditions that have been incorporated into later texts, that does not negate the later communities' affirmation of the truths in the texts. The later editors could have redacted out the earlier affirmations of the credo. For example, the P edition of the Decalogue in Exodus 20 has edited the Sabbath command to fit the context and theology of the community. The credo, however, has not been removed from the literary context.

While the credo has not been excised completely from the texts, it has been altered significantly. These alterations represent the different theologies of the different communities represented by the texts. For example, the JE source emphasizes the dramatic mercy and loving faithfulness of YHWH in Exodus 34; the D source places the burden on the people to keep the covenant commands; the two P sources record two different versions of the credo that each highlight different aspects of the relationship between YHWH and ancient Israel. This diversity of texts shows evidence of a complex understanding of how the nation was to relate to its Deity. Furthermore, the text shows that this diversity was also present throughout the different periods of ancient Israel's history. The presence of the different versions within the final form shows that there were different communities which could provide ideological support for keeping the different versions.

Furthermore, it seems that this final form also gives us clues as to the religious and political environment of the Persian Period that was responsible for the text as we now have it.[112] During this very tumultuous time in the life of the nation, there were certainly widely divergent views held by different communities concerning the nation's relationship with YHWH. There were some who emphasized that the covenant community must beware of again experiencing the wrath of YHWH and must keep the covenant commands in order for the nation to regain its independence under the leadership of YHWH. These groups within the community would have seized upon the emphases of the parallels of Exodus 20 and Deuteronomy 5. On the other hand, there were certainly those who held that the hope for the nation rested only in YHWH's unmerited grace. The enormity of the Persian Empire and scarcity of resources for the newly reconstituted nation would have been daunting. These communities would have found solace in the texts of Exodus 34 and Numbers 14 that give examples of YHWH's past faithfulness in spite of the unbelief and sinfulness of the people.

Second, the credo occurs in every important covenantal text. At every place in the narrative where the survival of the covenant is important, the credo appears. In Exodus 20, the covenant is initially established with the people. The covenant is reestablished in Exodus 34 after the people break the covenant with the worship of the Golden Calf. Again, in Numbers 14 the covenant is renewed by Moses' use of YHWH's own divine speech to inspire the reconciliation of relationship between God and the people. Deuteronomy 5 witnesses the reaffirmation of the covenant by the people as they prepare to enter the land.

---

112. For a survey of internal and external factors that would have allowed and caused the existence of multiple communities within post-exilic Yehud, see Berquist, *Judaism in Persia's Shadow*, esp. 3–22. Blenkinsopp also believes that the Pentateuch was crafted as a "civic constitution of the temple community of Judah under Persian rule" (*The Pentateuch*, 51). For another example of how the Torah would have functioned as a Persian period document, see Balentine, *The Torah's Vision of Worship*.

Walter Brueggemann argues that the credo is made of character-istic "God talk" to which the ancient Israelites reverted during times of crisis.[113] Brueggemann asserts that the credo of Exodus 34 is a core af-firmation of who God is that the people could always revert to when the context of "acute crisis" demanded a deep, core confession of the nature of the Deity.[114] Along with the credo, he also considers Hos 2:16–17 and Isa 54:7–10 as other instances of characteristic "God Talk."[115] While Brueggemann does not consider all four instances of the major parallels in the Pentateuch, his affirmation that the credo constitutes speech to which the nation looks when the times are dangerous and destabilizing is helpful. The appearance of the credo at the critical junctures in the narra-tive history of the covenant found in the Torah testifies to its importance. It is no mistake or coincidence that at these important junctures the credo occurs. Furthermore, these appearances early in the Tanak prepare the reader to be aware of future appearances.

Third, the importance of the place of the text can be seen in each pericope. In each occurrence, the credo either comes at the beginning of the pericope or at its climax. Beginnings and endings of texts are important. Boris Uspensky has argued that beginnings of texts help to bring into focus the narrative for the reader.[116] He states "[T]he narra-tive often begins with hints about the denouement of the plot which has not yet begun."[117] The importance of these beginnings have led literary theorists to call it the "primacy effect."[118] The primacy effect argues that the parts of the narrative that come first have more impact on the reader than material that appears in the middle of the narrative. In both Exodus 20 and Deuteronomy 5, the parallel of the credo occurs in the first part of the narrative. Both appearances are connected with the first two com-mandments on right relationship with YHWH that govern all the other commands. The other two appearances of the credo in the Torah also occur in climactic positions in the narratives. These ending positions are also important. Menakhem Perry also outlines the importance of texts

113. Brueggemann, "Crisis-Evoked, Crisis-Resolving Speech," 96–97.

114. Ibid., 95.

115. Ibid., 95–105.

116. Uspensky, *A Poetics of Composition*.

117. Ibid., 149.

118. Perry, "Literary Dynamics: How the Order of a Text Creates its Meaning," 53.

coming at the end of narrative, forming a textual frame.[119] These last things in the narrative have a tendency to provide the final lens through which the narrative is understood. With regard to beginnings and endings, he states "The literary text, then, exploits the 'powers' of the primacy effect, but ordinarily it sets up a mechanism to oppose them, giving rise, rather, to a recency effect."[120] In Exodus 34 and Numbers 14, the parallel to the credo comes in the final climactic portions of the text which witness YHWH's reconciliation with the people. In summary, the parallel appears in important locations in each of the four pericopes.

Fourth, each different occurrence of the credo witnesses manipulation and adaptation of the list of the attributes of YHWH to fit the narrative. The passages evidence a dialectical tension between the unmerited mercy espoused in Exodus 34 and Numbers 14 and the strong emphasis on works in Exodus 20 and Deuteronomy 5. The balance in the tension shifts in order to focus the covenantal responsibility on the most appropriate party in the narrative. The two instances where the credo is linked with the Decalogue emphasize the covenant role of the people by placing the wrath of YHWH first and significantly redacting the attributes of mercy. The two instances of the credo where YHWH forgives the people highlight YHWH's mercy as the defining characteristic.

Fifth, the emphasis on YHWH as a jealous God is closely tied to the credo in the Torah. YHWH's covenantal jealousy is associated with three of the four appearances of the parallels in the Torah. This close connection accents the intimate relationship between YHWH and ancient Israel. The credo comes as the intensity of the relationship increases with either covenantal (re)affirmation or forgiveness. The term becomes all the more common in Deuteronomy as the people are getting ready to enter the land.[121] In the narrative, the people are reminded to follow YHWH closely as they enter the land. Their survival in the hostile environment will be directly proportional to their commitment to their God.

---

119. Perry, "Literary Dynamics," 52–57.

120. Ibid., 57. See also Peter Rabinowitz, who asserts, "Readers assume that authors put their best thoughts last, and thus assign a special value to the final pages of a text" ("End Sinister: Neat Closure as Disruptive Force," 121–22).

121. Three of the five affirmations in the Torah that YHWH is a "Jealous God" come in Deuteronomy (4:24; 5:9; 6:15). The other two are used in conjunction with the credo (Exod 20:5; 34:14).

As noted above, YHWH's jealousy demands exclusivity on behalf of the people and promises preferential treatment to the nation.

Sixth, one other minor parallel to the credo exists in the Pentateuch. A minor allusion to the parallel comes in Deuteronomy 7. In 7:7–11, Moses reminds the people that YHWH has chosen them over the other nations, not because of their size, but because of God's covenant with the patriarchs and matriarchs. In Deut 7:9, Moses stresses that YHWH is the God "who keeps his covenant and loving faithfulness to the thousandth generation of those who love him." Contrarily those who hate YHWH will be repaid with destruction to their face (7:10). While this echo does not fully quote the credo as have the other instances, it again is used to remind readers that YHWH demands covenant loyalty.

3

Parallels of Exodus 34:6–7 in the Twelve

INTRODUCTION

Readers find four major parallels of Exod 34:6–7 in the Twelve. Joel 2:13 comes in a call for the people to rely on the mercy of YHWH and repent so that the nation may again experience the blessings of God; these blessings will cease the taunts from the other nations that ancient Israel's God is absent and that this absence has resulted in their poor fortunes. In the narrative of Jonah, the prophet uses the credo as an ironic lament of YHWH's compassion on the Ninevites (4:2) rather than reigning down destruction. The credo also appears in Mic 7:18–20 as the prophet rejoices with a concluding hymn of hope that God will once again show compassion to ancient Israel. In Nah 1:3, the credo comes as warning to the Ninevites that God's anger will soon be administered on them.

This chapter will argue that the parallels of the credo in this second section of the Tanak focus on YHWH's relationship with both ancient Israel and the other nations. The appearances of the credo in the Torah fixated on the intimate relationship between God and ancient Israel. In the Twelve, the lens widens to include the impact of YHWH's dealings with ancient Israel on the other nations and the ways in which God's workings with the other nations relate to ancient Israel. These parallels mark a middle point between the Torah's vision of YHWH's intimate relation to ancient Israel and the Psalter's vision of YHWH as king over the entire earth.

This chapter will explore the canonical location of these parallels within the Twelve. I will give special attention to diachronic layers within each book in which the credo occurs and within the overall redactional process of the Twelve. The chapter will begin with a brief overview of recent studies which take the books of the Twelve to be understood as a whole, rather than as twelve discrete units. The chapter will then move to an examination of each occurrence of the credo in the Twelve. The final portion of the chapter will be an examination of how the credo functions within the larger unit of the Twelve.

FORMAL STUDY OF THE BOOK OF THE TWELVE

The idea that the books of the Minor Prophets should be read as a whole can be traced back at least to the second century BCE as Jesus ben Sira prays for the "bones of the Twelve Prophets" to comfort the people of Jacob (Sir 49:10). In the Talmud, the Twelve are considered one book with only three blank lines dividing the books, one less than the four that divide books counted separately.[1] Later, some Rabbis held that the books of the Twelve should be kept together for pragmatic reasons—to keep the smaller ones from getting lost (B. Bat. 13b).[2]

Despite these ancient witnesses to the unity of the Twelve, only recently have scholars taken up the task of reading the Twelve in this way.[3] We will first examine some diachronic proposals by scholars, followed by synchronic analyses.

Diachronic Study of the Twelve

The study of the redaction of the Twelve is the main focus of diachronic concerns. The work of James Nogalski has dominated this area of study.[4] Nogalski's work examines how the different books of the Twelve came to be in their present location in the text and earlier collections than the Twelve. One of his major contributions to the discussion is that the book of Joel provides a "literary anchor" for reconstructing the redactional

1. Redditt, "Recent Research on the Book of the Twelve as One Book," 48.

2. Peterson, "A Book of the Twelve?" 4.

3. It is important to note that not all accept the unity of the Twelve. For some arguments against the unity of the Twelve, see Roberts, *Nahum, Habakkuk and Zephaniah*, 9; and Ben Zvi, "Twelve Prophetic Books or 'The Twelve,'" 125–56.

4. Nogalski, *Literary Precursors to the Book of the Twelve*; Nogalski, *Redactional Processes in the Book of the Twelve*; Nogalski, "Joel as a 'Literary Anchor' for the Book of the Twelve," 91–109. Nogalski's work also provides an abundance of synchronic connections between the books.

history of the prophets. He believes Joel to provide "dovetailing genres, recurring vocabulary, and the presumption of a 'historical paradigm' that 'transcends' the chronological framework of the dated superscriptions."[5] In this schema, Joel provides a key to interpretation in that it connects an older Deuteronomistic corpus of Hosea, Amos, Micah and Zephaniah with a later group composed of Haggai and Zechariah 1–8. That is, Joel was used as a bridge to bring together two earlier collections. With regard to the dovetailing, Nogalski finds themes present in both Hosea and Amos that Joel reworks into new meanings—a Zion context for repentance as opposed to the Northern emphasis of Hosea and Amos and an eschatological emphasis on judgment not present in the earlier two.[6] Recurring vocabulary which revolves around "agricultural fertility (or the lack thereof), the centrality of Judah and Jerusalem, the Day of YHWH, and theodicy" can be found in Joel and the remainder of the Twelve.[7] Again these themes were both taken up by the writers of Joel and redacted into the earlier works. The final place where Nogalski finds evidence for Joel as a "literary anchor" is in the way in which Joel transforms the earlier ideas of history present to make them into a more eschatological vision.[8] This new vision redefines the later history of the Haggai-Zechariah 1–8 layer added later. A final layer of Zechariah 9–14 and Jonah were the last additions to the Twelve.

While he is currently one of the leading voices within the study of the Twelve, Nogalski's work has not been accepted without reservations. For example, Aaron Schart sees a fourfold redaction of the Twelve that builds upon the Deuteronomic base.[9] Schart sees early versions of Hosea and Amos as composing an initial version of the Deuteronomic corpus to which Micah and Zephaniah were added.[10] A third stage came about as Nahum-Habakkuk was added and the fourth stage saw the addition of Haggai-Zechariah.[11] A fifth stage witnessed the insertion of

---

5. Nogalski, "Joel as a 'Literary Anchor,' for the Book of the Twelve," 92.

6. Ibid., 94–100.

7. Ibid., 100–104. Nogalski's earliest work focused on the redaction in of key words and phrases to bring unity to the Twelve ("The Use of Stichtwörter as a Redactional Unification Technique in the Book of the Twelve").

8. Nogalski, "Joel as a 'Literary Anchor' for the Book of the Twelve," 105–9.

9. Schart, *Die Entstehung des Zwölfprophetenbuchs*, 304–6.

10. Ibid., 128, 156–223.

11. Ibid., 234–51, 252–60.

Joel-Obadiah.[12] The text reached its final form when Jonah and Micah were added individually into the collection.[13] Like Nogalski, Schart believes that each layer saw a redaction of repeated themes and phrases into the texts. Schart's work is based upon common themes and motifs within the collections.

Byron G. Curtis has offered a reconstruction based upon the use of catchwords and common themes within discrete units in the Twelve.[14] Curtis, like Nogalski, argues for an early three book corpus made of Hosea-Amos-Micah (from the time of Hezekiah) to which was later added another three book set of Nahum-Habakkuk-Zephaniah (from the time of Josiah) sometime shortly after the fall of Jerusalem.[15] The redactors inserted various phrases linking the two and also added the book of Obadiah; Joel and Jonah were added independently after the exile.[16] Curtis finds the clue to the dating of the final unit of Haggai-Zechariah-Malachi in the Zion-Daughter oracle of Zephaniah 3 and its parallel in Zechariah 9. He uses a complex linguistic analysis of the ratio of Hebrew particles to other forms of speech to show that Zephaniah 3 and Zechariah 9 are later poetic redactions into their current prose context.[17] Curtis' work allows for a fuller appreciation of the theology of the final redactors of the Twelve. According to his reconstruction, these redactors "had a devoted theological and political interest in the restorationist program announced in the Zion-Daughter oracles" which had been inaugurated by Haggai and Zechariah, but was dropped by later generations.[18]

These three separate attempts at historical reconstruction show how difficult and tenuous any type of historical reconstruction can be. Two basic affirmations are important for our study. First, a core group of Deuteronomic prophets composed of Amos, Hosea, Micah and Zephaniah initially existed as stand alone units, all four of which contain Deuteronomic superscriptions that highlight the importance of the

---

12. Ibid., 261–82.

13. Ibid., 287–91, 297–303.

14. Curtis, "The Zion-Daughter Oracles," 166–84.

15. Ibid., 166–67.

16. Ibid., 167.

17. Ibid., 171–78. For a detailed discussion of how to find "prose-particle density," see Anderson and Freedman, "'Prose Particle' Counts of the Hebrew Bible," 165–83.

18. Curtis, "The Zion-Daughter Oracles," 183.

kings of Judah and the centrality of the South. Second, each addition to the core group was accompanied by intertextual insertions to tie the texts together. Scholars have accomplished significant work in this area. In addition to the work of Nogalski, Margaret Odel has argued that the idea of "prophets" is a theme that works its way through the Twelve and can be found in Hosea, Jonah, Zechariah and Malachi.[19] Biddle suggests that the terms "Israel" and "Jacob" give clues to a redactional history of the Deuteronomistic corpus of Hosea-Amos-Micah-Zephaniah.[20] John D.W. Watts suggests that Hosea 1–3 and Malachi form a "frame" which governs the overall meaning and structure of the Twelve.[21] The focus of this frame is that God's nature has not changed from the eighth century to the fifth century; God has always wanted to gather the broken nation; time has not changed YHWH's love toward the people.[22] The work of Odell, Biddle and Watts shows that as the corpus expanded, the themes and phrases of the later books were grafted into the other books.

Synchronic Study of the Twelve

Scholars have accomplished much in the way of finding synchronic, thematic unity in the Twelve.[23] Three works are closely related to the themes of this study. In 2000, Paul House argued that the Twelve shows a thematic development from judgment to hope when read as a unity.[24] In the first cluster of six books, House finds the major affirmation to be

19. Odel, "The Prophets and the End of Hosea," 160–69.

20. Biddle, "'Israel' and 'Jacob' in the Book of Micah," 146.

21. Watts, "A Frame for the Book of the Twelve," 209–17.

22. Ibid., 216–17.

23. While the bulk of scholarly work has been accomplished in the last twenty five years, earlier scholars recognized the unity of the Twelve. Franz J. Delitzsch detected passages that had similar agricultural imagery, similar descriptions of God and *Massa* headings in Nahum and Habakkuk ("Wann weissagte Obadja?" 92–93). Alfred Jepsen produced two articles that noted the similarity of the superscriptions in several of the books ["Kleine Beiträge zum Zwölfprophetenbuch," 85–100; "Kleine Beiträge zum Zwölfprophetenbuch II," 242–55]. Umberto Cassuto believed the repetition of בוא in Hosea 14; Joel 2, 4; Amos 1, 9; and Obadiah serves as a unifying feature ("The Sequence and Arrangement of the Biblical Sections," 1–6).

24. House, "The Character of God in the Book of the Twelve," 125–45. This article is built upon two of his older works—*The Unity of the Twelve* and "Dramatic Coherence in Nahum, Habakkuk, and Zephaniah," 195–208.

that God is the "God who warns."[25] While each book gives a different variation of this theme, they all are witnesses to the fact that YHWH wants to forgive. House sees in these texts many different characterizations of God, but "Each characterization undergirds the Twelve's belief to this point that judgment is not and never will be inevitable. The God who warns is the God who stands ready to heal and forgive."[26] Nahum, Habakkuk and Zephaniah form the next cluster of books. The idea that God is the God who punishes governs this triumvirate.[27] They are witnesses to the fact that YHWH will not tolerate sin—it must be eradicated. The final three books of the Twelve (Haggai, Zechariah, Malachi) are messages of exuberant hope that YHWH is the "God who renews."[28] This section was not a message that YHWH can or will renew, but that only YHWH can or will renew. The importance of House's work is the overall movement he sees from warning to judgment to renewal as is common in the other prophetic books and in that his schema rightly understands YHWH's dealings in the Twelve not only to concern Israel, but also the other nations.

The second major synchronic work to be considered is James Crenshaw's 2003 article "Theodicy in the Book of the Twelve," which argues that the conflict between faith and experience is the central theme that ties each of the Twelve together.[29] Within the Twelve, Crenshaw finds three different responses to the issue of theodicy—those that deny the problem exists, those that question traditional affirmations that the virtuous will prosper, and those that seek to redefine the character of YHWH. First in Zeph 3:1–5 and Hos 14:10, Crenshaw finds texts that assert that no discrepancy exists between the character of YHWH and the nation's predicament.[30] For example, Hos 14:10 affirms that the ways of YHWH are right and provide a place for the righteous to walk, but a stumbling block to the sinful. Second, Crenshaw finds within Malachi and Habakkuk a opposing call for justice that has fallen on deaf ears.[31] Malachi's oppo-

---

25. House, "The Character of God in the Book of the Twelve," 129–36.

26. Ibid., 137.

27. Ibid., 137–41.

28. Ibid., 141–44.

29. Crenshaw, "Theodicy in the Book of the Twelve," 175–91.

30. Ibid., 183–85.

31. Ibid., 185–86.

nents demand to know where this God is who keeps justice. In their view, "All who do evil are good in the sight of YHWH" (Mal 2:17).

Third, Crenshaw finds the most textual support in the Twelve for those that did not deny the problem or try to question traditional affirmations. This third group seeks to redefine the character of YHWH.[32] The first text he considers in this group is the parallels of the credo found in the Twelve. Crenshaw finds redefinition in the various contexts and theologies which emphasize the credo within the Twelve. In each of these contexts, however, the compassion of YHWH is affirmed while the punishing aspect is neglected. The only exception comes in Nah 1:2–3 as God vows to punish Nineveh because of exacting justice. Thus, in this instance the redefinition comes in the exaggerated emphasis on YHWH's compassionate nature. The second text in this third group is Amos' "liturgy of wasted opportunity" (4:6–12).[33] This liturgy offers a theodicy in which suffering is designed to stimulate repentance. The third text of this group is Amos 3:3–8 where YHWH is said to cause misfortune and assumes responsibility for evil. In summary, Crenshaw finds within the Twelve and these three different groups of texts a walk on the "razor's edge" between doubt and trust and between compassion and punishment that characterizes the issue of theodicy in the Twelve.[34]

In 1993, Raymond van Leeuwen made the case that in the final form of the Twelve the credo of Exodus 34 marks the issue of theodicy over against the punishment inflicted upon the nation in 722 and 587.[35] Van Leeuwen's analysis rests on the interconnections of the credo, Day of YHWH imagery and geographical play between north and south. His work emphasizes the occurrences of the credo in the first six books of the Twelve that gives the unit (and the overall Twelve) a wisdom focus.[36] This wisdom focus brings hope to the overall judgmental tone of the first books. Integral to the focus is a thematic frame set up by the liturgical ending of Micah (7:18–20) which contains the credo and the beginning

---

32. Ibid., 187–91.

33. Ibid., 190.

34. Ibid., 191.

35. Van Leeuwen, "Scribal Wisdom," 31–49. It should be noted that van Leeuwen's work is given in terms of the work of the final wisdom redactors of the Twelve, but his work outlines the contours of the final form of the text. It is for this reason that I have discussed it as a synchronic study.

36. Ibid., 33–34.

of Hosea. Following Spieckermann, van Leeuwen argues that the naming of Hosea and Gomer's second child (לֹא רֻחָמָה) is a dramatic reversal of the covenantal attributes of the credo and that the naming of the third child (לֹא עַמִּי) is a play upon the dialogue between Moses and YHWH in Exodus 32 about whose "people" Israel is.[37] This initial allusion and the liturgical ending give strong clues to the reader that the theological focus of the credo governs the Twelve. Van Leeuwen believes the sole appearance of the credo in the second half of the Twelve in Nahum 1 serves as a bridge between the two smaller units.[38]

Conclusions

The results of this brief overview of synchronic and diachronic approaches to the Twelve are multiple. First, while the Twelve contains enough narrative unity, literary cohesiveness and thematic connections to be considered one book, its composite nature cannot be denied. The texts may be considered one, but they do not exhibit the same type of unity that the books of the Torah or Deuteronomistic History contain. Second, because of this composite nature, diachronic and synchronic methodologies are more complementary than in any other section of the canon.[39] Information gained from redaction studies helps synchronic readings and vice versa. Third, the credo of Exodus 34 stands as a major text because of its use in literary connections and its thematic import for the issue of theodicy. The parallels of the text of the credo appear in four distinct places within the Twelve. Furthermore, the theological tension between YHWH's mercy and wrath evident in the credo provided a semantic field that was capable of supporting each of the different responses to the issue of theodicy present in the Twelve. Fourth, the issues of theodicy and YHWH's nature in the Twelve are connected more

37. Ibid., 35. Spieckermann makes a similar argument, but must assert that the tradition goes back to Canaanite El because he only thinks the credo to be exilic at the earliest ("Barmherzig," 3). Ruth Scoralick also suggests that the naming of the children of Hosea are echoes of the covenantal attributes (*Gottes Güte und Gottes Zorn*, 150–55).

38. Van Leeuwen, "Scribal Wisdom," 47–49.

39. Two major collections of essays shed light on this issue; in both of these works, a cursory look shows that diachronic and synchronic methods are tightly connected. See Nogalski and Sweeney, eds. *Reading and Hearing the Book of the Twelve*; and Schart and Redditt, eds. *Thematic Threads in the Book of the Twelve*.

intimately with the other nations than in the Torah. The credo of Exodus 34 stands as a major part of this theme in the Twelve.

APPEARANCES OF PARALLELS OF EXODUS 34:6–7 IN THE TWELVE

This section of the chapter will explore the appearances of the credo within the final form of the Twelve. As per the custom, I will first address matters diachronic, then the parallel's participation in Exod 34:6–7, before finally moving to a discussion of the place of the text within each book. This chapter will conclude with how appearances of the credo function within the final form of the Twelve and how the different constellations of texts in the MT and LXX might effect this function.

Joel 2

A parallel of the credo appears in Joel 2:13 in a call for the nation to repent and thereby divert the impending disaster to be meted out by locusts. The prophet calls the nation to change because of YHWH's merciful characteristics. The quotation begins the second half of the book which emphasizes a renewal of the nation in the future as the other nations are judged and the ancient Israelites are restored.

Diachronic Issues

Diachronic issues in Joel are notoriously difficult. As far back as 1879, Adalbert Merx called Joel the "problem-child" of Old Testament studies.[40] Scholars have dated the book anywhere from the eighth century to the second century BCE. For example, Karl A. Credner dated the book in the eighth century based on its placement in the canon with other eighth-century prophets.[41] More recently several scholars have followed his lead including E. J. Young.[42] At the opposite end of the spectrum, Bernhard Duhm argued that the final form of the text arose in the Maccabean period.[43] Duhm argues that the first half of the book (1:1—2:17) is from an

---

40. Merx, *Die Prophetie des Joel und ihre Ausleger von den ältesten Zeiten bis zu den Reformatoren*, iii–iv.

41. Credner, *Der Prophet Joel übersetzt und erklärt*.

42. Young, *An Introduction to the Old Testament*, 271.

43. Duhm, "Anmerkungen zu den Zwölf Propheten," 161–204.

early postexilic prophet, but the second half (2:18—4:21) was written as late as the Maccabean period. Others, such Hans W. Wolff, also argue for a composite nature, but he sees a date for the final form between 445 and 343 BCE.[44] Paul L. Redditt believes the book to have been written between 515 and 445.[45]

John Barton puts forth the most palatable argument.[46] Barton also sees a two part structure that divides the text after 2:27 with the earlier half coming sometime after the exile, and the text reaching its final form sometime in the 400's.[47] This final form is not simply an addition of the second half, but also bears witness to modifications to the original core. Two of Barton's arguments for a postexilic date are most convincing— Joel lacks the denunciation of national sin present in the eighth-century prophets and it contains a stock of images present in the postexilic prophets such as an outpouring of the Spirit (Ezek 32:7) and a gathering of the nations for judgment (Isa 34:1).[48] Barton's analysis also takes into account the multiple quotations and echoes of other texts present in Joel first catalogued by James Crenshaw.[49] Two other facts lead one to date the text after the exile: the text lacks any reference to kings which presupposes the end of the monarchy and Joel 4:1–2 seems to point to the end of the exile. It should be noted well, however, that these conclusions are tenuous at best. As much as any other text, Joel has defied diachronic analysis. While many follow the composite "two part" theory outlined above, this theory is in no way unanimous.

If the dualistic compositional nature posited above is correct, then it is difficult to determine the time in which the credo became part of Joel. Its place in the text could come from either the first writer of 1:1—2:27

---

44. Wolff, *Joel and Amos*, 4–5. Wolff finds these two dates by finding references to the wall of Jerusalem in 2:7, 9 (completed under Nehemiah's direction in 445 BCE) and the mention of Sidon in 4:4 (destroyed in 343 BCE). It should be noted that Wolff does not argue for a composite nature to the same degree as does Duhm. Wolff believes that most of the text could have been written by an original author, but it has evidence of later additions (8).

45. Redditt, "The Book of Joel and Peripheral Prophecy," 235. Redditt has a more detailed reconstruction of the growth of Joel than either Wolff or Duhm.

46. Barton, *Joel and Obadiah*.

47. Ibid., 17–18.

48. Ibid., 16.

49. Crenshaw, *Joel*, 27–28.

or any of the later redactors. The parallel, however, is an integral part of the narrative and theological pattern of chapter 2, which seems to be evidence that it is not a later redaction. Furthermore, it seems to be the case that the smaller pericope within which it functions as a call to lament (2:12–17) is not a later insertion. The text from 2:11 to 2:18 does not flow without the call to lament found in vv. 12–17. Additionally, the use of YHWH's jealousy for the covenant people in 2:18 connects the next section (2:18—3:5) with the call to lament.

In this context, Joel's use of the credo imagines that the punishment of the "locusts" (2:1–11) can be diverted by the people's repentance because YHWH is "gracious and compassionate" and ready to forgive the nation.[50] The only hope for the nation again rests in the compassion and grace of their deity. The impending crisis, be it natural or foreign, threatens the life of the nation who has very recently returned from the (near-) death of exile. The greatly compacted version of the credo in Joel would inspire hope that YHWH is the answer to the crisis.

Participation in Exodus 34:6–7

This parallel of the credo is the most truncated thus far in the canon. In fact, the parallel contains only three connections with the original— "Gracious and compassionate God," "Slow to anger," and "Great in Loving kindness." These three connections are significant enough to show connection with the original, but still demonstrate redaction in this context. Three issues come to the fore.

First, the text completely excises the second half of the credo that highlights YHWH's wrath. The text of Joel 2:13 stands as the first canonical appearance of the credo that ignores the tension of the original. The quotations of Exodus 20 and Deuteronomy 5 reverse the poles, but do not leave out any of the significant aspects as Joel does. Robert C. Dentan explains the discrepancy between the two texts by calling Joel's version a "more congenial" replacement of wrath with YHWH's proclivity to

---

50. Whether or not the "locusts" should be taken as a literal postexilic invasion by locusts is tangential. The important thing is that the nation currently faces an unbelievable punishment because of sinfulness. For an example of those who take the locusts to be literally locusts, see Allen, *The Books of Joel, Obadiah, Jonah and Micah*, 29–30; and Thompson, "The Book of Joel," 733–34. On the other hand, Graham S. Ogden and Richard R. Deutsch take the terms as metaphors that represent Israel's enemies (*A Promise of Hope—A Call to Obedience*, 19–20).

"relent from sending calamity."[51] On the other hand, Susan Pigott accounts for the disparity by looking at the broader context of Joel whereby Joel 1–2 provides the balance of the original credo.[52] She states, "Why would the prophet make reference to Yahweh's punishment of sin . . . since the entire first chapter and a large portion of the second were devoted to describing impending judgment?"[53] Furthermore, she holds that the wrathful aspects of Exod 34:7 may be given in a positive light in the final affirmation of the book in 4:21 that uses the common root of נקה which also occurs in Exod 34:7.[54] I find Pigott's analysis compelling.

Following Pigott's lead, it is important to note that the narrative context of this parallel of the credo comes not with the promise of punishment, as in Exodus 34 or Numbers 14, but in the actual severity of the locust plague. There would be no need to rehearse the harshness of YHWH's wrath because the people were currently experiencing it. This change is a significant theological statement by the community represented by Joel. For the first time, the community drastically recrafted the credo to fit the narrative and historical context. The canonically earlier manifestations of the credo certainly show modification, but never to this extent. By placing the wrathful attributes of YHWH in context rather than an explicit mention in the quotation of the credo, the community of Joel evidences a hermeneutic that moves away from the balance of the earlier quotations. This movement is not simply a result of a simple malicious deception, but could be a product of the community's being inundated by YHWH's wrath in their current setting. The apparent imbalance in the text would have provided needed balance for the historical community.

Second, the phrase "repents of evil" (נחם על־הרעה) is inserted in place of YHWH's wrathful attributes.[55] Again, this addition fits the literary context of Joel. The function of the credo in Joel is to admonish the people to turn from their sin and return to YHWH. The plague of locusts and harshness of their punishment has this returning as its end.

51. Dentan, "The Literary Affinities," 39.

52. Pigott, "God of Compassion and Mercy." Allen also believes that the context of the parallel mediates the use of Exod 34:7 (*The Books of Joel-Micah*, 80–81).

53. Pigott, "God of Compassion," 141.

54. Ibid., 141–42.

55. This occurrence and Jon 4:2 are the only parallels to use this language. They are, in fact, exact parallels. The significance of their connection will be discussed along with the discussion of the parallel in Jonah.

Wolff believes that the turning of the people must necessarily precede the repentance of YHWH, and that in this instance the credo "motivates the summons to conversion."[56] I find Wolff's assertion far more likely than that of others such as Raymond Dillard who assert that the attributes of YHWH such as gracious, compassionate, and slow to anger "culminate" in God's repenting from evil.[57] Dillard ignores the poetic context of the credo which is a call to repentance and lament. In this instance, Joel affirms the merciful aspects of YHWH's nature in order to draw the ancient Israelites back to YHWH.

Third, the merciful attributes of 34:6 are redacted and rearranged. The parallel in Joel 2:13 does not rehearse the fact that YHWH extends "loving kindness to the thousandth generation" or that God takes away "iniquity, transgression and sin." The reason for the omission of these attributes is difficult to ascertain, without again looking at context. The next verse holds that God may or may not remove the punishment currently administered on the community. The interrogative "who knows" (מִי יוֹדֵעַ) looms large over all of the prophet's talk about YHWH's mercy. The community sees itself in such a tenuous position that their lament and repentance may or may not cause God to have mercy. Thus, the attributes that emphasize the removal of sin and extension of mercy to thousands of generations would not have been the most appropriate to rehearse.

For the same reason, the attributes rehearsed are appropriate for the immediate context. The community would have been in dire need of God's grace and compassion.[58] God's immeasurable loving kindness for the nation would have also been immensely important for the ravaged nation.[59] The inclusion of YHWH's slowness to anger is problematic. This attribute is difficult in the literary context, considering the wrath which the nation is currently experiencing. The only explanation for this attribute is that the prophet wanted to remind the ancient Israelites that YHWH's wrath is not hastily given or without warning; God has punished the nation because they were unfaithful and left YHWH.[60] Wolff

56. Wolff, *Joel and Amos*, 49–50.

57. Dillard, "Joel," 280.

58. The order of חָנוּן and רַחוּם have been reversed from the original.

59. YHWH's אֱמֶת was also removed in this parallel.

60. Interestingly, the only explicit sin mentioned in the book is that of drunkenness in 1:5. Dillard believes that this absence of specific sins shows that the book of Joel was

proposes that the phrase shows that YHWH is "free in God's own anger."[61] Just as God patiently waited for the nation to change, the divine anger can be stopped at any time. God's slowness to anger is mentioned to show that their punishment is deserved, but can be reversed at any time.

Participation in the Larger Context

The parallel of the credo found in Joel 2:13 stands in a pivotal place in the narrative. The most prominent feature of its location is that it is part of the lament that moves the book from the description of YHWH's wrath present in the first half of the book to the future hope expressed in the second half of the book. The use of שׁוּב "return" marks the lament of 2:12–17. Because of the lack of concrete sins named, it is uncertain what the people should leave. Crenshaw believes that it shows the people were worshipping other gods.[62] Duane A. Garrett calls it simply a turning away from sin.[63] While it is vague from what the ancient Israelites were turning, either sin, idols or some other thing at odds with their relationship to YHWH, it is definite that their loyalties are to be again given to YHWH.[64]

The imperative is given twice in both 2:12 and 2:13. The manner in which the people should return follows the first occurrence in 2:12—with fasting, weeping and rending of the heart. The reason why the people should return follows the second occurrence in 2:13—YHWH is a gracious and compassionate God and may actually hear their lament. These two charges to the people make up the Call to Lament in 2:12–14 which is then acted upon in 2:15–17 with actual fasting and weeping.[65]

This Call to Lament serves as a fulcrum on which the overall structure of the book hinges. Prior to 2:12 the text is marked by destruction and wrath; after 2:11 the text tells of a time when YHWH will again give life and blessings. Part of this new life is that YHWH will again be "jealous" for the nation (2:18). For the fourth time, YHWH's covenantal

originally a liturgical text used in national laments ("Joel," 280–81). He continues, "The fact that no specific transgressions are named broadens the number of situations to which this liturgy could be applied (281).

61. Wolff, *Joel and Amos*, 50.

62. Crenshaw, *Joel*, 189.

63. Garrett, *Hosea, Joel*, 347.

64. Barton, *Joel, Amos*, 77.

65. See also Dillard, "Joel," 282, who divides the text in this way.

jealousy is connected with the credo (Exodus 20; 34; Deuteronomy 5). The result of God's passion for the people is that the destructive impact of God's wrath will be reversed. The crops devoured by the locusts (1:4, 7, 10, 12, 17) are restored. The harshness of destroyed grain, dried up wine and failing oil (1:10) will be forgotten because YHWH is sending grain, wine and oil to fully satisfy the people (2:19). This dramatic reversal all stands as a result of YHWH's "returning" jealousy.

Another important aspect of the parallel's place in the narrative comes as its thematic echoes frame the book. The book begins with generation imagery. The fathers of the elders are said never to have seen or experienced destruction to the degree like that currently meted out on the nation (1:2). At the same time, the children will tell of the harshness of the current time to their children, and they will retell it to their children to the third generation from the current fathers and mothers (1:3). Wolff sees in these verses a futuristic move from prophecy to apocalypticism.[66] One does not need to follow Wolff. Rather, the generational imagery is not a move forward, but hearkens back to the old creedal traditions of Exod 34:6–7. As noted above, the parallel of the credo in Joel is void of this generational imagery. In the dramatic reinterpretation of 1:2–3, it is no longer YHWH's loving kindness that is given to future generations, but now their heritage is the memory of God's wrath.[67] Joel ends, as noted by Pigott, with another dramatic reinterpretation of the credo—God will "pardon" the guilt of the people (4:21). Interestingly, both sides of the frame echo in ways opposed to the meaning of the original—the generations to come will tell of YHWH's wrath, but at the end YHWH will pardon their guilt.

Lastly, it should be noted that YHWH's return of compassion and jealousy for the people will result in the nations being judged. Part of the actual lament among the people was that they no longer wanted to be an object of scorn among the nations (2:17). The other nations, after seeing the harsh judgment on the people, taunted the ancient Israelites with the invective, "Where is your God?"[68] They assumed that destruction equaled absence rather than punishing presence.

66. Wolff, *Joel and Amos*, 26.

67. The text of 1:3 could also echo the omitted sections of Exod 34:7.

68. For the prevalence of the question of divine absence, both by the ancient Israelites and their enemies see the work of Joel S. Burnett, "The Question of Divine Absence in Israelite and West Semitic Religion," 215–35.

In Joel 2:18, the second part of YHWH's answer to the lament offered and the people returning is that never again will God make them an "object of scorn" to the other nations. Again in 2:26–27, the prophet gives a double exclamation that no longer will "my people" be shamed. The whole of Chapter 3 is given to the concrete details of the judgment upon the nations. Twice the text mentions that the nations will be gathered and brought down to the mythical "Valley of Jehoshaphat" (4:2, 12). The mythical name is an onomastic play on "YHWH's judgment" (יהושׁפט) rather than the name of an actual locale. Wolff states nicely, "The prophet knows the geographical location as little as he knows an exact date for the final conflict of Yahweh with the nations."[69] The prophet imagines a dramatic future reversal of the judgment upon the people and a turning of that judgment upon the nations who have taken delight in the wrath heaped upon ancient Israel. The book ends with exuberant hope that matches the harshness of the opening chapters.

After the study of the use of the credo in Joel, four summary statements can be made:

1. In the historical community of Joel, the credo functioned as a call to repentance based upon the forgiving nature of YHWH. The prophet envisioned this repentance changing the overall course of the fate of the nation.

2. This version of the credo is the first canonical expression to completely emend one of the two theological poles.

3. The credo appears in a pivotal juncture in the poetic sequence in the call to repentance. After the lament based upon YHWH's loving kindness, the overall mood of the book changes from judgment to hope.

4. Echoes of the credo frame the book, in addition to the pivotal place of the credo, which shows the overall importance of Exod 34:6–7 and its tradition for Joel.

Jonah 4

The credo's function in Jonah 4 is the most peculiar of all its Old Testament parallels in that the prophet laments because of YHWH's gracious and compassionate nature. After the Ninevites' dramatic repentance, the

---

69. Wolff, *Joel and Amos*, 76.

prophet becomes depressed because of YHWH's compassion on the Ninevites because the prophet thought that their nature demanded judgment. In a book that is marked by satire, the use of the credo exists as another ironic statement.[70]

Diachronic Issues

Few scholars consider the narrative of Jonah to record an actual historical event and even fewer believe it is likely to have been written during the time of the Assyrians.[71] The book of Jonah lacks any strong historical markers such as is present in the eighth-century prophets in the Twelve. The text also contains many anachronisms from the Persian Period, such as the participation of domestic animals in mourning and the connection of kings and nobles in making decrees.[72] In light of this absence of historical markers, the most common method used to date the book of Jonah centers on finding the genre of the text.[73] Some have found the book to be an example of allegory.[74] In the allegorical view, Jonah represents ancient Israel. Jonah's journey into and out of the great fish symbolizes the nation's exile and return to the land. In the end, Jonah is freed to be a prophet to the Ninevites who symbolize the nations. In this view, the text would be an early postexilic work and would have encouraged the ancient Israelites as they returned to the land—it would have motivated them as a nation to see their current situation as providential. Others have seen the text as a parable.[75] When read as a parable, the text is meant to counter the hostile xenophobia of the Ezra-Nehemiah camp and to show that YHWH's covenantal attributes are available to all the nations. In this view, the text could have been written anytime between 600–200 BCE.[76] Finally, others have taken the book to be a didactic prophetic narrative

---

70. For the use of irony and satire in Jonah, see Ackerman, "Satire and Symbolism in the Book of Jonah," 213–46; Good, *Irony in the Old Testament*, 39–55; Holbert, "'Deliverance Belongs to Yahweh!'" 334–54; and Marcus, *From Balaam to Jonah*, 93–160.

71. For those that consider a historical account of an eighth-century prophet, see H.L. Ellison, "Jonah," 362–63; and Alexander, *Jonah*, 51–77.

72. Allen, *The Books of Joel, Obadiah, Jonah and Micah*, 186.

73. Pigott, "God of Compassion and Mercy," 144–48.

74. For example, Smith, *The Book of the Twelve Prophets*, 498–507.

75. For example, Smart, "The Book of Jonah," 872–73; and Bewer, "A Critical and Exegetical Commentary on Jonah," 4.

76. Pigott, "God of Compassion and Mercy," 145.

meant to teach the ancient Israelites.[77] This view is the most appealing as it can incorporate the aspects of the other models. A didactic narrative can contain satire, allegory and other narrative genres; the text need not be limited to any one genre.

Even if one decides upon a genre (allegory, parable, or didactic narrative), the exact dating of the text is difficult. Any of these three options could theoretically function at any time after the exile. In any case, however, the most that can be said is that Jonah is postexilic. In this historical light, the credo would have shown that God's compassion and mercy were completely available to the other nations. The end of this revelation could either be that the postexilic nation must actively go and prophesy of YHWH's goodness (allegory) or it could be that they should be open to outsiders within their community (parable).

One possible help in dating Jonah comes in its relation to Joel. With regard to the parallel of Exod 34:6–7, the context of Jonah shows that the prophet was quoting Joel (discussed below). Jonah 3:9 is also a quotation of Joel 2:14. Assuming that Jonah quoted Joel, Jonah can be dated to sometime after Joel in the 400's. More importantly, when the two texts are held side by side, the dramatic tension between postexilic communities over the inclusion/exclusion of foreigners is apparent.

Participation in Exodus 34:6–7

The quotation of Exod 34:6–7 in Jonah 4 is an exact parallel of the quotation in Joel 2. The parallel even includes the added phrase from Joel 2, "And repents from evil." Pigott again holds that the quotation can be explained by context commenting, "The formula is equally appropriate within the context of Jonah even though it is cited for a completely different purpose."[78] Pigott's comments neglect some of the key literary aspects of Jonah, however. First, Jonah completely ignores the wrathful characteristics of YHWH's nature present in 34:7. This omission is remarkable because of the fact that these characteristics are the ones which the character Jonah most wanted YHWH to exhibit. Furthermore, it is unusual for a worshipper to lament the fact that the deity has acted in characteristic fashion. A normal lament is voiced because the deity's

77. Pigott opts for this view ("God of Compassion and Mercy," 145). See also Simundson, *Hosea, Joel, Amos, Obadiah, Jonah, Micah*, 258–59.

78. Pigott, "God of Compassion and Mercy," 153.

actions have resulted in a current circumstance of the worshipper which are not desired.[79] It would have been completely within reason for Jonah to lament that YHWH did not act wrathfully toward the Ninevites. Second, the context does not explain why Jonah would have omitted the aspect of YHWH's extension of loving kindness to thousands and the phrase "taking away iniquity, transgression and sin" from his lament. This removal of the sinfulness of the Ninevites forms the actual reason for his lament. Pigott rightly states that "Jonah's accusation was that in his indiscriminate compassion Yahweh had been unjust."[80] The removal of sin and extension of loving kindness would have been natural components of Jonah's accusation.

A more plausible scenario is that Jonah is dependent upon Joel. Many have read the book of Jonah as a response to the theology of Joel.[81] The quotation of the credo in Jonah stands as deliberate reinterpretation of the exclusivistic theology of Joel. Thus the parallel of the credo should be interpreted in light of the original, but also in light of the quotation in Joel which it seeks to counter. Thomas Dozeman, who does not prefer one diachronic trajectory of interpretation, believes that the two should be understood as "anthological interpretations of covenant renewal."[82] He believes that the two texts are explorations of "latent or potential meanings concerning the implications of covenant renewal for both Israel and the nations."[83] Stated simply, Jonah uses the same text to show that God's mercy is open to all the nations, not only the ancient Israelites.

Participation in the Larger Narrative

Readers of the text of Jonah are surprised at two things—the actions of Jonah and the actions of the Ninevites. The prophet initially rejects the call of YHWH to go to the Ninevites and later gives a halfhearted message to the nation. Surprisingly, the Ninevites repent, including even their

79. E.g., Psalms 10 and 13; Jer 20:7–18.

80. Pigott, "God of Compassion and Mercy," 154.

81. Allen, *The Books of Joel, Amos, Obadiah, Jonah and Micah*, 228; Childs, *Introduction to the Old Testament*, 424; Fishbane, *Biblical Interpretation in Ancient Israel*, 346; Wolff, *Studien zum Jonabuch*, 68–71.

82. Dozeman, "Inner-Biblical Interpretation of Yahweh's Gracious and Compassionate Character," 221–23. Dozeman also sees the covenant-renewal narrative of Exodus 32–34 linking the two texts.

83. Ibid., 222.

animals, and turn to YHWH. The text is full of surprises and irony. The credo's appearance in the text helps to answer both of these questions.

The actions of Jonah are strikingly disobedient for what one might consider appropriate for the "son of faithfulness" (בֶּן־אֲמִתַּי—Jon 1:1). Jonah's characterization throughout the narrative is negative. Jonah refuses to go to Nineveh and promptly heads in the other direction toward Joppa.[84] He utters inappropriate speech such as a thanksgiving psalm while still in the fish, an assertion of faith in YHWH even while fleeing and a denunciation of God's merciful attributes; even his eventual prophecy does not come out of repentance, but simply because he cannot resist YHWH.[85] Raymond Person has catalogued some of the ways that contemporary readers have tried to accommodate for this disconnect between Jonah's status as a prophet and his refusal to go to Nineveh by supplying extra information such as geographical, spiritual or psychological factors.[86] Jonah refused because of the distance to be traveled (750 miles over a desert), Satan's murmurings in his ear, or for fear of the Ninevites who were known for their harshness. I contend, however, that the reader finds the reason for narrative disconnect with the appearance of the credo in Jon 4:2.

The credo does not effectively clear up all of the dissonance as Jonah offers it as a lament. Amazingly, Jonah's anger kindles even as YHWH's abates. The content of Chapter 4 comes as a stark surprise to the reader.[87] As Jonah bursts into lament because of the potency of his message, the peculiarity and impotency of the prophet is again emphasized. The lament is all the more surprising because Jonah offered a thanksgiving while he should have lamented (Jonah 2); now the prophet laments when he should have offered a prayer of thanksgiving. The credo does supply the reader with the reason why Jonah has acted in such a peculiar manner—he knows of YHWH's compassion and does not want it extended to the Ninevites.

---

84. Allen calls Joppa the "ideal destination in the escape plan Jonah devises" because of its distant location (*The Books of Joel, Amos, Obadiah, Jonah and Micah*, 205).

85. Marcus, *From Balaam to Jonah*, 157. Marcus believes that, "Jonah is depicted throughout the story as a virtual caricature of a prophet" (157).

86. Person, *In Conversation with Jonah*, 137–38.

87. Terrence Fretheim calls the content "Psychologically almost incomprehensible" (*The Message of Jonah*, 118).

Jonah's anger intensified as the thing he feared most actually came to pass. In fact, the ironic extension of his wrath because of YHWH's lack of wrath and extension of compassion causes the prophet to want to die (4:3). A death wish is nothing unusual for a prophet, but the others have usually risen from different circumstances. Moses asks for death rather than to face the ungrateful Israelites looking for meat and again undermining his leadership (Num 11:10–15). Elijah asks for death after the defeat of the prophets of Baal on Carmel has no results on the attitude of Ahab and Jezebel (1 Kgs 19:1–9).[88] Jeremiah laments his birth because the harshness of the message of YHWH is too difficult to carry to the people (Jer 20:7–19). Jonah's request is all the more ironic when considered in light of his recent experience with YHWH's compassion to save his life after being consumed by the great fish. It is the very compassionate nature that Jonah is lamenting about that has saved his life and allowed his current tantrum.

The credo also functions in the narrative to bring to light how the foreigners' actions fit into the story. In several of the texts, those from the other nations act appropriately even while Jonah's actions are otherwise. The obedience of the sailors and the Ninevites sharply contrasts with that of Jonah. While the storm raged and Jonah slept, the captain went below deck to ask Jonah to call upon "your God" for help (1:6). Later, the sailors offer sacrifices and fear YHWH after God quiets the sea when Jonah is thrown overboard (1:14). Most remarkably, the whole city of Nineveh repents when they hear the message of Jonah (3:6–9). The king of Nineveh even echoes the voice of the prophet Joel with a quotation of Joel 2:14, "Who knows, [God] may turn and repent" (Jon 3:9)?

The combined effect of Jonah's disobedience and the obedience of the foreigners makes this radical new interpretation of the credo seem more appropriate. The irony of Jonah's lament over the extension of YHWH's mercy and loving kindness to the Ninevites becomes even more ironic when compared to the actions of those in the nations. Jonah has continually been disobedient, but was extended YHWH's mercy without repentance; Jonah now laments that the Ninevites were offered mercy after their repentance. The credo offers YHWH's covenantal attributes to

---

88. Allen believes that the portrait of Jonah here is a parody of the words of Elijah (*Books of Joel, Amos, Obadiah, Jonah and Micah*, 229). The author could have had any of the "righteous" prophets (Moses, Jeremiah, or Elijah) in mind in this instance.

another nation for the first time in the canon. The irony of the narrative reaches a climax with Jonah's lament. The climax provides resolution for the reader as Jonah's disobedience is explained because of YHWH's compassion and the Ninevites are offered compassion because of YHWH's character.

After the above discussion, four summary affirmations can be made about the character of the credo in Jonah 4.

1. The credo in Jonah comes as a direct response to the use of the passage in Joel 2.

2. This formulation of the credo is a direct quotation of the parallel in Joel 2.

3. For the first time, the credo is used to show YHWH's compassion is available to other nations.

4. The credo supplies important information that heightens the irony of the narrative, namely why Jonah is a disobedient prophet and why the Ninevites are not destroyed.

Micah 7

The book of Micah records three separate summons for the people to "hear" the word of YHWH (1:2; 3:1; 6:1) that destruction is immanent. Each summons to hear about YHWH's immanent destruction ends with a proclamation of hope (2:12–13; 5:3–15; 7:7–20). The parallel to the credo comes as the final doxology in the last proclamation of hope (7:18–20). YHWH's compassionate and forgiving attributes stand as the final reason the nation has hope for the future. The final doxology which centers on the credo of Exod 34:6–7 stands as a reminder that the severe economic injustices and idolatry for which the people are guilty, can be pardoned.

Diachronic Issues

There is a general consensus among scholars that the book of Micah underwent significant redaction to reach its current state and is not completely the product of the eighth-century prophet.[89] Critics have ap-

89. For a summary of diachronic research on Micah, cf. Willis, "Fundamental Issues in Contemporary Micah Studies," 77–90; Jeppesen, "New Aspects of Micah Research," 3–32; Jacobs, *The Conceptual Coherence of the Book of Micah*, 14–45.

proached the text using traditio-historical criticism, form criticism and rhetorical criticism.[90] The most common technique used to analyze the book has been redaction criticism as several layers are present in the text.[91] The text itself is easily delineated into three major sections marked by the triple summons to "hear" (1:2; 3:1; 6:1), but these do not represent clearly distinct time periods.[92] It is generally believed that the basic form of the first three chapters originated during the eighth century with Micah of Moresheth, but was later emended and redacted.[93] The text of Micah 1–3 shows later interpolations in places like the exilic/postexilic nature of 2:12, which asserts that a remnant of Jacob will be brought back together like sheep in a pen. Micah 4–5 came as the result of exilic and early postexilic redactional activity. The chapters' imagery of deliverance and return would have been welcome messages to the exilic nation (4:1–8; 5:6–8). The eschatological vision of a great temple in 4:1–5, to which all nations will pilgrimage, shows that this layer of redaction was completed sometime before the dedication of the temple in 515.[94] A third redactional layer is present in Micah 6:1–7:6, which originated sometime after the exile, but the exact date is hard to pinpoint.[95] This layer gives no clues which demand a certain historical setting.

---

90. For an example of the traditio-historical approach, see Beyerlin, *Die Kulttraditionen Israels in der Verkündigung des Propheten Micha*, who argues that the cult was the primary setting for the book. For a form-critical approach, see Stansell, *Micah and Isaiah*, who attempts to show ways in which Micah breaks from the tradition of Isaiah. Stansell only analyzes the first three early chapters of Micah. For an approach that uses rhetorical criticism, see Shaw, *The Speeches of Micah*. Shaw thinks that the rhetorical form of the speeches of Micah can be used to find their historical context. Interestingly, he dates all of the speeches to the time of Micah.

91. E.g., Wolff, *Micah*; Lescow, "Redaktionsgeschichtliche Analyse von Micha 1–5," 46–85 and "Redaktionsgeschichtliche Analyse von Micha 6–7," 182–212; Nogalski, *Literary Precursors*, 123–25.

92. Allen, *The Books of Joel, Amos, Obadiah, Jonah and Micah*, 257–60, also divides the text in this way. A fourth imperative form of the root (שָׁמַע) also appears in 3:9, but is simply a parallel to 3:1.

93. E.g., Allen, *The Books of Joel, Amos, Obadiah, Jonah and Micah*, 251; Mays, *Micah*, 23–24; Wolff, *Micah*, 26.

94. Wolff, *Micah*, 26. See Anderson and Freedman, who date Micah 4–5 after Micah 6–7 [*Micah*, 17–20].

95. Mays, *Micah*, 30.

The fourth and final layer of the text came with the insertion of the liturgical materials of 7:7–20 that contain the parallel to the credo.[96] Modern study of these final verses has been led by Hermann Gunkel.[97] Gunkel's article argued that the pericope is made of four components—a "Dirge of Zion" (7:7–10), a "Divine Oracle" (7:11–13), a "Dirge of Israel" (7:14–17) and a "Hymn" (7:18–20).[98] He locates this final section during the early postexilic period during the time of third Isaiah and believes that it was used "as a 'liturgy' by different singers on one of the 'days of dule' in Jerusalem."[99] The dating of the passage is difficult as the pericope contains few concrete historical markers, but its themes and style show it to be different from the rest of Micah. A *terminus ad quem* may be found in 7:11 which looks forward to a great eschatological day when the walls of Jerusalem will be rebuilt and places the passage sometime before the walls were constructed under Nehemiah.[100] This final doxology most likely completed the book sometime at the end of the sixth century.

Regarding the historical place of the credo in this enunciation, the postexilic nation would have been comforted by YHWH's compassion and grace. Earlier than either Joel or Jonah, this proclamation of the credo is the earliest of the occurrences of the Twelve. The "nations" oppressing the ancient Israelites will be made ashamed and their power will be taken from them (7:16). This turn in events will happen because YHWH has not forgotten the covenantal love for the battered nation (7:20). This instance of the credo proclaims that hope is on the horizon.

Participation in Exodus 34:6–7

The quotation of the credo in Micah 7 is the most loosely quoted of all the major parallels within the canon.[101] I take 7:18–20 to be a hymn based upon the text of Exod 34:6–7 and have chosen to include it as a

96. Even Allen, who maintains that almost all of Micah originated with Micah of Moresheth, believes 7:8–20 to be a very late insertion (*Books of Joel, Amos, Obadiah, Jonah and Micah*, 251).

97. Gunkel, "The Close of Micah," 115–50.

98. Ibid., 142.

99. Ibid., 147. Wolff, *Micha*, 219, follows Gunkel in this dating, as does Mays, *Micah*, 30.

100. Wolff, *Micah*, 219.

101. Pigott does not include Micah 7 in her discussion of major parallels ("God of Compassion and Mercy").

major parallel for the following reasons.[102] First, three parallels of the different sections of the credo appear in 7:18–20 although each has been greatly changed from the original. The text maintains that YHWH "takes away iniquity" and passes over "transgression" that begins the passage and would have reminded the reader immediately of the credo with its paraphrasing of YHWH's ability to remove sin from the covenantal relationship. Second, the text asserts that YHWH "does not stay angry forever" (לא־החזיק לעד אפו). I take this assertion to be a restatement of the original "slow to anger" (ארך אפים). Finally, vocabulary from the original inundates every section of the hymn in which Micah 7 proclaims YHWH to delight in showing *loving kindness*, to return *compassion* to the nation, to subdue their *iniquities* and to cast their *sins* into the sea. The relationship will be restored because of the divine remembrance of *faithfulness* to Jacob and *loving kindness* to Abraham. The hymn focuses on imagery from the original.

The overall effects of this recrafting of the credo to this hymnic form are twofold. First, the hymn emphasizes the positive attributes of YHWH more than the original. For example, in the hymn God does not simply "take away" the people's iniquity, transgressions and sin. Instead four verbs are associated with YHWH's "taking away" of the people's unrighteousness, the original "take away" (נשא), "pass over" (עבר), "subdue" (כבש), and "cast" (תשל) are used.[103] This addition of verbs moves the rhetorical weight toward YHWH's actions rather than the people's sin. Another way that the text places more emphasis upon YHWH's compassion than the original is by the positive emotions that the text gives to YHWH—not only does God extend loving kindness, but here "delights" in showing loving kindness to the people. The same could be said about the hymn's move from "slow to anger" to the affirmation that God "will not remain angry forever." The hymnist wanted to emphasize the point that God does not seek to be angry, but rather merciful. Last, the hymn connects these verbal attributes with concrete aspects of YHWH's behavior. The verbal form תהן can denote either past or future. If "Jacob" and "Abraham" are taken literally, then the text could be a recollection of

102. See Mays, who also believes the hymn to be based upon the credo (*Micah,* 167).

103. The verb "to pass over" describes YHWH's action in Exod 34:6 as God moves in front of Moses.

past faithfulness to the patriarchs. On the other hand, the terms could be metaphorical to symbolize the nation, as is often the case, which would mean the text is a look forward to acts of mercy given to the people.[104] This ambiguity adds to the effect on the reader and could call to mind both past and future. YHWH's past faithfulness to the people can be used as a model of the deity's future actions toward the "remnant of God's inheritance" (7:18). Overall these three modifications in the credo over-emphasize the merciful aspects of YHWH's character making it one of the most positive manifestations of the credo in the canon.

Several aspects of the old credo have been omitted from this new hymn. Of the merciful attributes, the only one not reworked in the new hymn is that YHWH's loving kindness extends "to thousands." This theme may have been covered with the past look at God's faithfulness to Jacob and Abraham, but it is never explicitly mentioned as are the other aspects of the compassionate pole. This omission is significant in that it would have been thematically appropriate in the hymn that celebrates YHWH's compassion and faithfulness to the nation.

The most noticeable revision, however, is the complete emendation of YHWH's wrathful attributes. For the first time in the canon, there is no mention of YHWH's wrath with any significant reason for the omission. In each of the parallels in the Torah, some aspects from each pole are retained; in Joel, echoes of the wrathful attributes frame the book; in Jonah, the wrathful attributes are omitted as the book is a direct and deliberate quotation of the passage in Joel 2.[105] The reason for the omission may lie, as Pigott has asserted about other texts, in the fact that the larger context of the book is dominated by YHWH's wrath.[106] The writer of the hymn sought to give the people hope for the future based upon YHWH's mercy. The wrathful aspects of YHWH's nature would have been inappropriate in the historical and narrative context of Micah.

---

104. Anderson and Freedman, *Micah*, think that the inversion of the normal order of "Abraham . . . Jacob" shows that the text is referring to the original patriarchs and that the nation has already received whatever אמת and חסד connote (599). On the other hand, Mays, *Micah*, remarks, "Abraham and Jacob are used as characterizing names for the people as the corporate objects of YHWH's election (the former only here in the Old Testament)" (168).

105. See the earlier discussions of Joel and Jonah for further explication.

106. E.g., Pigott, "God of Compassion and Mercy," 141, 154–55.

Participation in the Larger Narrative

The location of the parallel in Micah stands in a place in the narrative which is significant in three different contexts.[107] Reading synchronically, the text can be read as a conclusion to the pericope of 7:7–20. It also functions as a conclusion and summation of Micah 6–7. Finally, and most obviously, it serves as a liturgical conclusion to the book as a whole. The functions of the parallel will be examined as a part of each of these three contexts.

First, the hymn based upon the credo forms the fourth and final section of the pericope from 7:7 to 20. At first noted by Gunkel, the text is composed of four different sections. Gunkel found a thematic balance in the texts between lament and salvation oracle as the four sections alternate between lament and praise. In Gunkel's view, the hymn provides final liturgical praise in response to the dirges of Zion and Israel in 7:7–10 and 7:14–17. Mays states the balance nicely, "The first piece speaks of a *deliverance* which the enemy will *see*. The second promises and details that *deliverance*. The third prays for the deliverance to occur as renewal of the people and as revelation which the nations shall see. Then in the final unit the 'theology' of the whole is stated in praise of God's forgiveness."[108]

In addition to contributing to the liturgical balance of the pericope, the hymn also brings together much of the theology of the final section. Two questions are present in the text. In 7:10 the other nations have taunted the people by asking, "Where is the Lord your God?" This question is answered in the final hymn with the exclamation, "Who is a God like you?" The hymn also answers the questions of the laments theologically. The lament of 7:9 acknowledges that the sins against YHWH have resulted in the current state of the nation. In fact, the speaker of the lament readily accepts the punishment, "The rage of YHWH, I must carry because I have sinned." The hymn balances this acceptance of punishment by noting that Jerusalem and ancient Israel's only hope lie in the redemptive acts of YHWH. The poetic celebration of this mercy is so startling that Wolff believes this hymn to be the only occurrence of YHWH's forgiveness of sin in song as opposed to God's power and glory

---

107. Ehud Ben Zvi comes close to mirroring this assertion by holding that the passage serves "double duty" by providing closure to the book and to 7:7–20 (*Micah*, 173).

108. Mays, *Micah*, 152.

(Ps 89:7), redemptive acts (Pss 71:19; 77:14; 86:8) or faithfulness to the covenant (1 Kgs 8:23; Isa 44:7).[109]

The parallel also serves as a fitting conclusion to Micah 6–7. The chapters begin with YHWH's bringing a lawsuit against ancient Israel which ends with the oft quoted assertion that all God requires is for the people to act justly, to love loving kindness and to walk humbly (6:8). The second half of Micah 6 outlines the judgment upon the city because of their sin (6:9–16). Micah 7 begins with a lament over the misery of living under the wrath of YHWH (7:1–6). The section steadily builds in intensity, from the disappointment of not finding any food when hungry (7:1), to the feeling of impotence when living in a land with evil judges (7:3–4), and then finally to the horror of not even being able to trust the members of one's household (7:5–6).

David Hagstrom notes that when reading Micah 6–7 the "most striking feature" is the abrupt change in mood in 7:7, which shifts from doom to hope.[110] Hagstrom asserts that 7:7 is the climax of the narrative and that the hymn of 7:8–20 serves to resolve the tension of the passage.[111] In this climax and resolution, Hagstrom finds the central theme of YHWH's faithfulness to the covenant people. Another approach is taken by Shaw, who suggests that 7:1–7 functions as an epilogue and forms the end of the section, ending the book with a "vivid, haunting picture of a moral wasteland."[112] Shaw gives no account for how the book functions as a whole; rather he focuses on the probable historical date of each of Micah's speeches.[113] In the final form of Micah, however, the words of

---

109. Wolff, *Micah*, 229.

110. Hagstrom, *The Coherence of the Book of Micah*, 103.

111. Ibid., 103. Hagstrom makes a very good case that the "Jacob" of 7:20 forms an envelope structure with the mention of "Israel" in 6:2 (117). In Micah 1–5 the terms are used often, but only appear twice in Micah 6–7. Hagstrom's work shows that Micah 6–7 can stand alone as an individual unit.

112. Shaw, *The Speeches of Micah*, 187. Shaw bases his assertion that the section is an epilogue on what he calls the "four functions" of epilogues—they should incline the audience toward the speaker and against opponents; they should maximize evidence for the speaker's argument and minimize detractions; they should emotionally effect the audience; and they should refresh the reader's memories (187). Shaw thinks that 7:1–7 fulfills all four of these functions.

113. Shaw (ibid., 225) believes 7:8–20 to have been composed after 722 BCE and the capture of Samaria. This historical context explains the abrupt change between the two sections.

7:1–7 only carry the penultimate word. The deplorable state of the nation is not the final judgment of YHWH, but there is mercy and compassion in the future for the nation as expressed in the hymn of 7:8–20. The balance of the literary units tempers the harshness of 7:1–7. The text roots this future hope of the nation in YHWH's past redemptive acts. In the opening accusations against the nation, YHWH reminds the nation who brought them out of Egypt (6:4). The final section looks forward to a time when those scattered will return from Assyria, Egypt and all over the earth (7:12). Micah 6–7 ends with hope that YHWH will again have mercy on the nation and call them out from their oppressors.

The parallel of the credo and the pericope of 7:7–20 also serve as a very fitting conclusion to the book as a whole both theologically and linguistically. The pericope contains many of the broad theological ideas of the previous chapters such as lament and future hope. Ben Zvi sees many different "reverberations of significant wordings" between these final verses and the remainder of the book.[114] In 7:14, the text speaks of YHWH's "shepherding" the people, while in 2:12 the prophet also looks to the time when the remnant of Jacob and Israel will be brought together like "sheep in a pen." The beginning of the hymn in 7:18 also mentions this "remnant" of 2:12 and 5:7. One of the charges brought against the people is that they have cheated their kin of their "inheritance" (2:2), while 7:18 celebrates God's pardon of the divine "inheritance" (7:18). Other examples exist such as in 1:12 where the inhabitants of Maroth "wait" for relief, but YHWH sends disaster; but in 7:7 Jerusalem "waits" for YHWH its savior.[115]

Another lexical connection between the beginning of Micah and the parallel of the credo comes in the name of Micah. The book begins with the superscription that the texts were written by Micah (מיכה) of Moresheth which is a shortening of the question "Who is like YHWH?" (מי כ־י יהוה). With this naming, a theme of the book is set as an attempt to answer the question of which other gods are like the God of ancient Israel. Throughout the book, the theme is reemphasized as the people

114. Ben Zvi, *Micah*, 179. The following "reverberations" are taken from Ben Zvi.

115. For other examples of reverberations, see Luker, "Doom and Hope in Micah," 212–17 and Willis, "*Structure* of Micah 3–5 and the Function of Micah 5:9–14 in the Book," 191–214. See Hagstrom for thematic links between Micah 1–5 and 6–7 (*The Coherence of Micah*, 115–24).

are criticized for their idolatry and practice of improper worship.[116] The question's final answer comes with the hymn based upon the credo, which begins with the question, "Who is a God like you" (7:18)? The remainder of the hymn answers the question by explicating YHWH's compassionate nature. In a similar vain, Wolff sees the hymn as a *liturgical* response to the name of the book.[117] The final form of Micah guides the community toward worshipful response to the question "Who is like YHWH?" This liturgical response is that the attributes of Exod 34:6 are what separates YHWH from the other gods.

Each of these lexical "reverberations" reshapes the old themes and turns the theology toward the positive compassionate nature of YHWH. The appearance of the hymn at the end of Micah reshapes the theology of the entire book. The book begins with the appearance of YHWH in wrath, but now ends with a hymn that centers on God's mercy.[118] Wolff states the change in this way, "Micah's message of judgment does not have the final say; instead—after all the suffering brought by this judgment—the message of salvation, proclaimed since Deutero-Isaiah (cf. Isa. 51:1–3), has the final word. Here that message is taken up and sung as a hymn."[119] Childs stresses the importance of the fact that the book ends in worship, saying, "The liturgical ending again offers a profoundly theological interpretation of how the community of faith understands itself in relation to the prophetic proclamation."[120]

In the final analysis of Micah, the book moves readers to faith-filled trust in the compassion of YHWH as their only answer. The all too recently experienced wrath stands in direct opposition to the hope that YHWH's compassion will soon come. Childs states the tension evoked by the use of the credo nicely, "The community of faith is assigning its role as the worshipping body, standing in between God's judgment and salvation, and possessed by both memory and anticipation."[121] The credo

116. E.g., Mic 1:7; 5:12–13.

117. Wolff, *Micah*, 228.

118. Mays, *Micah*, 152. For the importance of beginnings in texts, see Uspensky, *A Poetics of Composition*, 149; and Perry, "Literary Dynamics," 53. For the importance of endings in narratives, see Rabinowitz, "End Sinister: Neat Closure as Disruptive Force," 121–22.

119. Wolff, *Micah*, 231–32.

120. Childs, *Introduction to the Old Testament*, 437.

121. Ibid.

ends the book with a resounding note of hope and anticipation that YHWH's wrath has ended.

In conclusion, there are four summary statements to be made regarding Micah's use of the credo:

1. In Micah, the credo stands as a dramatic expression of hope for a community who has recently returned from exile to find their city broken and destitute.

2. Of the major parallels of the credo, this manifestation evidences the most lexical and theological manipulation in the canon. This manipulation resulted in a doxological hymn.

3. The significance of the place of the parallel is important on three different levels—as an ending to the pericope of 7:7–20, as a conclusion to Micah 6–7 and as a doxology for the entire book.

4. The overwhelming positive nature of the credo as well as its position in Micah shifts the theological emphasis of the book from judgment to salvation.

Nahum 1

In Nahum 1, a parallel to the credo comes as a stark warning that the Ninevites will not be able to forego YHWH's wrath. The parallel comes at the very beginning of the book and sets the tone for it. The text places the most emphasis of any canonical parallel on YHWH's wrath. It is also the only occurrence of the credo that is directed solely toward another nation.

Diachronic Issues

Finding a general date for the book of Nahum revolves around three separate issues. First, many hold that a *terminus a quo* can be found in the reference to the fall of Thebes in 663 BCE.[122] In Nah 3:8–10, the prophet declares that Nineveh will be no better than Thebes who seemed impregnable, but ultimately met a very harsh end. Most hold that Nahum could not have been written before 663 BCE because the fall of Thebes is mentioned in the past tense. Second, a *terminus ad quem* is found in the

---

122. E.g., Bailey, "Nahum," 137; Roberts, *Nahum, Habakkuk, and Zephaniah*, 38; Spronk, *Nahum*, 12.

predicted future fall of Nineveh which occurred in 612 BCE. Again the book, which revolves around the future fall of Nineveh, would have carried far less narrative weight if Assyria's capital city had already fallen.

Within this five-decade timeframe (663–612), several different ideas exist for when to date the book. Roberts holds that the text was written sometime between 640 BCE and 630 BCE to provide ideological support for Manessah's revolt against Assyria.[123] Walter A. Maier, positing a date of about 654 BCE, argues that the text was written before the power of Assyria began to wane.[124] Barker tentatively places the book sometime shortly before 627 BCE when the forces of ancient Israel were weak and Assyria's power was high.[125] Spronk holds the text was most likely written about 650 BCE when the image of defeated Thebes would still have been fresh in the minds of the people and would have elicited attention from the Ninevites.[126] Any variety of other ideas exist within the dates of 663–612 BCE to date the text.

A third factor must be considered when dating the book of Nahum. The text of Nah 2:1 is remarkably similar to Isa 52:7. Both texts contain the phrase, "The mountains of the feet of him who brings good news, who announces peace." These texts are the only two to use the phrase in the entire Old Testament.[127] Nogalski thinks this scarcity of quotation shows that one of the two texts is dependent upon the other, rather than both drawing from a common source.[128] He does not believe that there are strong indications of the trajectory of the quotation. If Nahum borrows from Isaiah, then the text of Nahum must be assumed to be postexilic.[129] The trajectory could certainly move from Nahum to Isaiah, but no definitive proof exists to solidify either case. Nogalski believes that

---

123. Roberts, *Nahum, Habakkuk and Zephaniah*, 39.

124. Maier, *The Book of Nahum*, 30–31.

125. Bailey, "Nahum," 139.

126. Spronk, *Nahum*, 13.

127. See Coggins, "An Alternative Prophetic Tradition?" 81, who sees a close relation between Isaiah and Nahum, notably Nah 1:4 and Isa 33:9, 50:2 and Nah 1:15b and Isa 52:1b.

128. Nogalski, *Redactional Processes*, 97.

129. Schultz, *Das Buch Nahum*, 15–20, takes the book to be postexilic. Haupt, "The Book of Nahum," 1–53, takes the book to be from the Maccabean period because of its liturgical nature.

the intertextuality with Isaiah 52 stands as a reason why "a more definitive date has yet to gain unqualified acceptance."[130]

Further adding to the difficulty of dating is the apparent redaction
in the acrostic hymn of Nah 1:2–8. The acrostic is composed of a couplet
that begins with each of the succeeding letters from א to כ. The main
diachronic issue relating to the credo comes as the parallel is inserted
under the א couplet. The difficulty lies in the fact that the א section of
the acrostic is not made of one couplet, but three making it the only letter to receive three couplets. Roberts believes that this expansion is not
a mark of later exilic redaction, but of "an expansion that seems to give
added emphasis to the opening of the acrostic. "[131] Roberts sees this expansion as either coming from the prophet himself or another source.
Nogalski holds that the text is a later addition and is emblematic of the
larger redactional processes that resulted in the final form of Nahum.[132]
Jörg Jeremias believes that the additions which contain the parallel to the
credo are part of a redactional layer of the late exile/early post exile.[133] As
noted above, van Leeuwen believes it to be part of a final wisdom layer
of the Twelve.

Another option is simply to assert that the poem is not an acrostic.
Michael Floyd argues that the text of 1:2–10 is neither an acrostic nor
liturgical, but should be classified as "prophetic interrogation."[134] Floyd's
argument is based upon the fact the acrostic is only half of the alphabet
and even then has several textual interruptions. The א, ד, ז, and י lines
do not begin with the appropriate letters. That is of the acrostic, only
seven of the eleven lines match the literary pattern. Others have argued
similarly to Floyd.[135]

The most creative alternative belongs to Spronk, who sees an initial
line-acrostic before the alphabetic acrostic begins.[136] The first letters of

---

130. Nogalski, *Redactional Processes*, 99.

131. Roberts, *Nahum, Habakkuk and Zephaniah*, 48.

132. Nogalski, *Redactional Processes*, 103.

133. Jeremias, *Kultprophetie und Gerichtsverküdigung in der späten Königszeit Israels*,
16–19.

134. Floyd, "The Chimerical Acrostic of Nahum 1:2–10," 436–37.

135. See Allis, "Nahum, Niniveh, Elkoch," 69; Haldar, *Studies in the Book of Nahum*,
15–33; Maier, *Nahum*, 149–95; and Smith, *Micah–Malachi*, 71–76. For support of seeing an acrostic, see Nogalski, *Redactional Processes in the Book of the Twelve*, 101–2.

136. Spronk, *Nahum*, 25.

the verse lines in 1:2–3a spell out the personal pronoun אֲנִי, then 1:3a begins and ends with the name of YHWH. Spronk sees in this pattern a play on a Mesopotamian line-acrostic that also begins with a personal pronoun (Akk. *anaku*), then the author's name.[137] In Nahum, the author inserted YHWH's name instead of his own because that is where he found his inspiration. After this line-acrostic, the alphabetic acrostic begins in 1:3a after the name of YHWH with אֶרֶךְ. Spronk's proposal is interesting, but unlikely because one must rearrange the words to begin the larger alphabetic acrostic.

Ultimately, I think that the proposals of Nogalski and van Leeuwen are most probable for the following reasons. First, it is highly unlikely that Nahum would have *almost* attempted an acrostic.[138] The "corruptions" in the text likely stem from later redactions. Second, the chronological markers of the fall of Thebes and Nineveh do not necessarily limit the text to the seventh century. The text could have been reused by later communities as a warning to the superpower of the day that their reigns were tenuous. Third, the canonical position of Nahum immediately after Micah supports the idea of the credo being redacted into the acrostic later. The redactors of Nahum could have inserted the credo at the beginning of Nahum to connect it with the final hymn of Micah. I would add, however, that I do not believe the final hymn of Micah and the added couplet to the Nahum acrostic to be part of the final redaction by a single redactor. The two parallels are far too different to come from the same hand. In this interpretation, Nineveh and Assyria would have been symbolic of any major superpower which supposes that it does not owe allegiance to YHWH. The use of the credo, in this context, would have reminded the exiled nation that YHWH's wrathful side can also be turned toward the other nations.

Participation in Exodus 34:6–7

The parallel of the credo found in Nahum 1 has three connections with the original. Both use the phrases, "slow to anger," "surely not acquitting

137. Ibid. See the "Babylonian Theodicy," *Texte aus der Umwelt des Alten Testaments*, III/1, 143–57) and a prayer from Ashurbanipal to Marduk (*Texte aus der Umwelt des Alten Testaments*, II/5, 765–68) for an example of this type of line-acrostic.

138. I find this argument of Nogalski to be the most convincing (*Redactional Processes in the Book of the Twelve*, 102).

the guilty," and use of the name "YHWH." Several other similar themes to those found within the credo are in Nahum 1, but no other direct quotes can be found.[139] This occurrence of the credo is the only one in which all aspects of YHWH's nature are used in a negative way, in a completely negative context. The phrase "slow to anger" is usually used to emphasize YHWH's propensity to withhold punishment. In Nahum, it is used to show the Ninevites that God's anger has been a long time coming and will not be thwarted. In the original, "slow to anger" is paired with the affirmation that YHWH is "great in loving kindness." Nahum changes the רב־חסד to גדל־כוח.[140] Nahum replaces YHWH's loving kindness with strength.

Pigott sees the combination of slowness to anger and great strength as a sign of YHWH's "controlled judgment," which will be used to enact righteousness.[141] This shift toward controlled judgment completely overhauls the impact of the credo. Roberts correctly understands Nahum's reinterpretation, "Nahum's emphasis, however, is quite different. While he acknowledges this traditional confession about the nature of Yahweh, he shapes the statement to support his own borrowed portrait of Yahweh as an enraged God of harsh vengeance."[142] With this emendation, the redactor shows himself to be a crafty manipulator of the original. With this slight change, the tone of the credo is reversed. The completion of the picture of YHWH's vengeance comes with the reaffirmation that God will in no way clear the guilty.

Julia O'Brien suggests that the threefold repetition of YHWH's vengeance (נקם) in 1:2 sets the tone of the entire section.[143] This triple affirmation of YHWH's vengeance would have given the reader a clear impression of the tone of the passage. On the other hand, Spronk sees a contradiction between the two affirmations of YHWH's slowness to anger and judgment on the guilty which he thinks are intended to counterbalance each other.[144] In my opinion, he fails to see the way that the

---

139. Pigott, "God of Compassion and Mercy," 166.

140. The difficulty of this change can be seen in the *Biblia Hebraica Stuttgartensia* note to revert back to חסד.

141. Pigott, "God of Compassion and Mercy," 16–67.

142. Roberts, *Nahum, Habakkuk and Zephaniah*, 50.

143. O'Brien, *Nahum*, 48.

144. Spronk, *Nahum*, 37.

redactor reinterprets the old tradition in a completely new light. There is nothing graceful or compassionate in this confession; YHWH's wrath will not be thwarted.

In addition to the changes made to craft the credo completely focused on vengeance, this parallel is also the only occurrence of the credo which expresses God's wrath on another nation. This abrupt change to focus on wrath comes because ancient Israel is no longer the recipient of these attributes; the credo places Nahum under YHWH's domain. Bailey sees connotations of kingship in the emphasis on vengeance because of the power and legitimacy needed to exert one's will onto the other nation.[145] This use of the credo places the other nations, namely Nineveh, firmly under YHWH's reign. The other use of the credo relating directly to another nation (Jonah 4) is mediated through Jonah and is an extension of YHWH's mercy to the Ninevites. In Nahum, YHWH's wrath is given directly by YHWH.

Participation in the Larger Context

This section of the chapter will argue that the parallel to the credo in Nahum, like the other parallels of the credo in the Twelve, appears in a significant location in the narrative. Two important aspects of its place will be considered. First, it is notable that the credo comes at the very beginning of the book as an introduction to the acrostic of Nah 1:2–8. Childs suggests that these verses set the tone for the entire book. He states, "The first key to the canonical understanding of Nahum's prophecy is provided by the role of the introductory psalm of 1:2–8."[146] These verses set the tone for and provide a summary of the entire book—Assyria will be punished, but Judah will be restored to power. Each of these themes is present within the credo. The punishing aspect of the credo is immediately apparent when reading the text. The triple enunciation of vengeance and the overwhelming wrathful nature of this version of the credo begin the book in such a way that YHWH's intentions are clearly portrayed. This vengeance dominates the rest of the book.

On the other hand, the announcement of YHWH's wrath does have secondary positive implications. This punishment means restoration for Judah. In fact, the section begins with the oft-accompanying epithet

145. Bailey, "Nahum," 167.
146. Childs, *Introduction to the Old Testament*, 443.

"Jealous God" (1:2).[147] The epithet stresses the intimate relation of YHWH and ancient Israel. This intimacy will result in a dramatic change in the nation's fortunes. Despite the overarching theme of YHWH's vengeance, there are several glimpses into the positive aspects of punishment on the Assyrians for ancient Israel. Nah 1:12 states that Judah will no longer be the object of YHWH's affliction and Nah 2:2 holds that Jacob's splendor will be restored. The book holds that the judgment placed upon Assyria bodes well for ancient Israel's future.

Considering the above, four summary conclusions can be made regarding the use of the credo in Nahum 1.

1. This parallel of the credo would have reminded the exiled ancient Israelites that YHWH's wrath would soon be delivered to the nations which have oppressed them.

2. This parallel is the only occurrence in the canon which focuses only on YHWH's wrathful characteristics.

3. The place of the parallel at the beginning of the book helps to set the tone for the entire book by explicitly stating YHWH's wrath on Nineveh.

4. The parallel is again connected to the epithet of YHWH as a "Jealous God." This connection implicitly signals positive tones for the ancient Israelites as their enemies are to be punished.

CONCLUSIONS

The final section of this chapter will outline some conclusions, both diachronic and synchronic, based upon the above analyses. These conclusions will move from the micro level and the use of the credo in the different books to the macro level and the use of the credo in the Twelve.

Microlevel Conclusions

Several summary diachronic affirmations can be made regarding the use of the parallels of Exod 34:6–7 in the books of Joel, Jonah, Micah and Nahum. First, it was decided that each of these four were from a time

---

147. As with the occurrences of "Jealous God" in the Torah, idolatry is again mentioned as a sin. In this instance, however, it is the idolatry of the Ninevites that has provoked YHWH's jealousy (1:14).

within a century of the end of the exile. Joel's use of the credo can be dated to sometime in the early fifth century; Jonah was written shortly after Joel as a reaction to his exclusive claims; Micah's final form originated in the late sixth century; lastly, the final form of Nahum including the acrostic hymn, comes from the middle to late fifth century. This analysis has shown that the post-exilic community of ancient Israel was anything but monolithic.

In fact, each of the different communities represented by the different books has manipulated and shaped the pre-exilic credo to support different theological perspectives. The central issue around which the use of the credo revolved was the relationship of the other nations to ancient Israel and YHWH. How was the nation to deal with the national disasters of 722 BCE and 587 BCE? In this regard, I am in complete agreement with the analysis of van Leeuwen who sees within these texts an affirmation that "On the one hand, YHWH is free to exercise his forgiveness and mercy toward any who repent and, on the other, that he will not be held forever hostage to the evil of the wicked. "[148] He believes this freedom to be an attempted explanation of theodicy.

Speaking synchronically, the parallels of the credo in the Twelve exhibit far more lexical and theological diversity than those of the Torah. Joel presents the credo as a reason why the ancient Israelites should repent; Jonah laments the extension of YHWH's gracious attributes to the Ninevites; Micah celebrates YHWH's graciousness with a hymn based upon the attributes of the credo; Nahum offers the wrathful attributes as a warning to Nineveh. The different appearances of the credo run the gamut from emphasizing the wrath of YHWH to a hymnic celebration of God's compassionate attributes. Each of these different manifestations of the credo, except for Jonah, shows intentional crafting to conform it to the overall theology of the book. As opposed to the appearances of the credo in the Torah, none of the occurrences in the Twelve maintain the bipolar theological tension and balance of the original. Each opts to emphasize either compassion or wrath at the exclusion of the other. Pigott has gone to great lengths to try to find echoes of the excluded attributes in the text.[149] Pigott's conclusions are not always entirely convincing,

---

148. Van Leeuwen, "Scribal Wisdom," 49.

149. Pigott, "God of Compassion and Mercy," 131–66.

such as her explanations of a lack of compassion in Nahum or finding wrath in Jonah.[150]

In the parallels of Joel 2 and Nahum 1, the credo is again joined with the naming of YHWH as a "Jealous God." These two appearances present a similar theme in radically different ways, but both result in the same outcome. In Joel 2, YHWH's jealousy will be aroused only after ancient Israel's repentance. The outcome of this arousal of YHWH's passion is that the nation will again receive blessings (Joel 2:19), while the armies of the nations to the North will be defeated (Joel 2:20). In Nahum 1, YHWH's jealousy is intimately connected to Divine vengeance. The text is ambiguous and could either be an affirmation of YHWH's jealousy for ancient Israel or for the Assyrians. This jealousy will result again in punishment for the nation of Assyria (Nah 1:8–11), but a restoration of blessings to Jacob/Judah (2:2).

Most important, the credo appears in significant locations in each book, just as in the Torah. In Joel, the parallel's location functions as a call to repentance and serves as a break between the harshness of the first half of the book and the exuberant hope of the second half. In Jonah, the parallel comes at a climactic position toward the end of the book that allows the reader insight into Jonah's ironic behavior. In Micah, the final verses of the book offer a hymn based upon YHWH's compassionate attributes. It was shown that this final section contains lexical and thematic connections to the earlier portions of Micah which reshape the final theology of the book towards a hope for the future. In Nahum, a parallel begins the book with an announcement of YHWH's wrathful attributes. These attributes foreshadow the remainder of the book which promises destruction for Nineveh. In each case, the credo appears in an important lexical and theological location.

Macrolevel Conclusions

The analysis of the credo also provides some insight into how the Twelve may have been ordered. First, our examination of the credo provided significant insight into the diachronic ordering of Joel and Jonah. Our analysis showed that Jonah followed Joel based upon the fact that the quotation of the credo in Joel "fits" the narrative context. The fact that

---

150. Pigott, "God of Compassion and Mercy," 152–54, 165–66.

Jonah uses the same exact quotation, but that it does not coordinate with the narrative in the way that Joel does shows Jonah to be a response to the exclusivity of Joel.[151]

Contrary to the opinions of Nogalski and van Leeuwen, a single redactor was not responsible for the incorporation of different parallels of the credo into the Twelve. The four appearances of the credo within the Twelve are far too different to have come from a single redactor. Van Leeuwen believes the placement of the parallels forms a coherent framework between the books that compose the Twelve. It is more likely that if the redactors inserted the credo at significant junctures for unity, then they would have been more careful to harmonize the parallels. The fact that van Leeuwen takes the final form to have come from one community further undermines the diversity present within the parallels.[152] Nogalski's work shows the particularity with which the final redactors placed key terms and phrases at the seams and other significant locations to unify the Twelve. The radical differences between the parallels show them to have originated from different hands.

In the final analysis, the most that can be said about the formation of the Twelve, based only upon evidence gleaned from our analysis of the parallels, is that there was some intentional placement of the books. This placement is most apparent in the junction of Micah-Nahum. The late dating of the acrostic of Nahum 1 shows that it very well could have been composed in order to provide cohesion between the Hosea-Micah corpus and the Nahum-Zephaniah group. Nogalski's work has shown how Nahum 1 could have been redacted to mesh not only with the rest of Nahum, but also with the remainder of the Twelve.[153] The major objection to this view is that the only *stichwort* held in common between Mic 7:18–20 and Nah 1:2–3 is "anger" (אף).[154] This loose connection may have not been enough to connect the two texts. I think, however, that this "loose connection" gives evidence of a common tradition behind

---

151. It is common in redaction criticism of the Twelve to hold that Jonah was a late addition. E.g., Kapff, "The Perspective on the Nations in the Book of Micah," 289.

152. Van Leeuwen, "Scribal Wisdom," 49.

153. For other ways in which the acrostic of Nahum 1 uses other imagery from the Twelve see Nogalski, *Redactional Processes in the Book of the Twelve*, 115–17; and Nogalski, "The Redactional Shaping of Nahum 1 for the Book of the Twelve," 193–202.

154. Micah 7 uses the simple "anger" (אף), while Nahum 1 uses the euphemistic "long of nose" to convey slowness to anger (ארך אפים).

both texts which the parallels would have drawn to readers' minds. I attempted to show that the redactor of Nahum who inserted the credo was creative in his crafting of the parallel.

The redactor's ingenuity not only connected Nahum with Micah, but the parallel of the credo also serves as an appropriate introduction to the Nahum-Habakkuk-Zephaniah corpus. This manifestation of the parallel serves as a fitting beginning to these three books which emphasize the "God who punishes." This harmonizes with Nogalski's theory that Nahum 1 was intentionally crafted to provide *stichworts* with other parts of the Twelve. In my opinion, no further affirmations of the formation of the Twelve, based upon evidence found in the parallels to Exod 34:6–7, can be made.

This analysis of the credo is also helpful when focusing on the overall shape of the Twelve. When read synchronically, the reader would be struck by the varied responses generated to "the nations" by the parallels to the credo. The overall message of the Twelve regarding YHWH's relationship to nations other than ancient Israel is ambiguous. Each of the four gives a different valuation of YHWH's interaction with the other nations further complicated by each parallel's monolithic nature as opposed to the bipolar contrasts of the original. Jonah 4 shows that YHWH's compassion is extended to the nations, while Joel 2, Micah 7, and Nahum 1 emphasize God's covenant relationship with ancient Israel at the expense of the other nations.

Regarding the overall synchronic movement of the Twelve, as was noted at the beginning of the chapter, the text moves from judgment to hope as one reads through the books. Ronald Clements argues that the form of prophecy as a whole stresses YHWH's "message of coming salvation."[155] Clements' study does not apply this rubric to the Twelve as a whole, but the pattern can be found here. The credo's appearances in the first half of the Twelve all focus on YHWH's compassionate nature in contexts of repentance (Joel 2, Jonah 4, and Micah 7). This use supports House's idea that Hosea-Micah focuses on the "God who warns" as each of the parallels are associated with turning from sin.

Striking within House's understanding of the Twelve is that there are no appearances of the credo within the final three books of the Twelve which portray YHWH as the "God who renews." The attributes of YHWH

---

155. Clements, "Patterns in the Prophetic Canon," 44.

would have matched the theme of YHWH's movement from punishment to compassion. Within the overall movement of the Twelve, this use of the credo would have been very appropriate. In the Torah, two uses of the credo focus on movement from punishment to compassion (Exodus 34; Numbers 14). A "compassionate" reworking of the credo would have matched the overall positive nature of Haggai-Zachariah-Malachi.[156]

Contrary to its function in the Torah, three of the parallels of the credo in the Twelve serve as a call to repentance or an assurance that YHWH will be merciful if repentance comes. In the Torah, two appearances come in the context of the forgiveness of sin (Exodus 34; Numbers 14), while two appearances warn of YHWH's punishment for idolatry (Exodus 20; Deuteronomy 5). In the Torah, none of the appearances are intended to initiate repentance, but instead focus on YHWH's actions and attributes. In the Twelve, the parallels emphasize the actions of the nations or ancient Israel as a response to YHWH. The intimate covenant partnership between YHWH and ancient Israel also changes as the parallels open the relationship to the other nations.

Another difference in the location of the parallels in the Twelve is that they do not occur in significant places in the texts in the same manner as the parallels of the Torah. While I have approached the Twelve as a unity, I do not think that it exhibits the same level of unity that the books of the Torah exhibit. For this reason, it is difficult to make the same assertion about the locations of the parallels on a macro level as was made about the location of the parallels in the Torah.

Regarding this unity, there are some significant differences in the constellation of books of the LXX from the MT—while the last six books remain in the same order, the first six are Hosea, Amos, Micah, Joel, Obadiah and Jonah. In this order, Micah's hymnic celebration of the compassionate attributes of YHWH comes as the first parallel of the credo in the Twelve. The radical compassionate nature of the hymn concludes and provides balance to the first three books of the LXX—all three of which are wrathful eighth-century prophets. The second appearance of the credo in the LXX comes in the exclusivist claims of Joel, which is quickly balanced by Jonah's claims.[157] Jonah is the sixth book and comes

---

156. This lack of parallels is also evidence that a single redactor did not insert the credo into the Twelve as a unifying feature.

157. The two books are only divided by the twenty-one verses of Obadiah.

immediately before Nahum in the LXX. This location of Jonah emphasizes the theological tension between the two books which offer radically
different proposals of the future of Nineveh.

In sum, the order of the books of the LXX concentrates the appearances of the credo far more than the order of the MT. The four major
parallels appear in a string of five books. Furthermore, the location of the
parallels within the books intensifies the effect on the reader. In the order
of Micah-Nahum, the parallel concludes Micah, stands as a key component of Joel, is absent in Obadiah, forms the climax of Jonah, and finally,
introduces the visions of Nahum. The only book not to have a parallel of
the credo is short, and the four parallels come in the most compressed
way. This constellation of books highlights the parallels of the credo far
more than that of the MT.

4

Parallels of Exodus 34:6–7 in the Psalter

INTRODUCTION

R eaders find three major parallels of the credo in the Psalter. This
chapter will argue that these appearances of the parallels emphasize
YHWH's reign over the entire earth. Psalm 86 uses the credo to assert
that YHWH's kingship is marked by goodness and forgiveness. The credo forms a central aspect of Psalm 103 which extols the overwhelmingly
positive character of YHWH's rule over all. In Psalm 145, the credo forms
the substance of the praises of all creatures for God the King. In addition
to the importance of the credo in the individual psalms, special attention
will also be given to the fact that these three psalms are located near the
end of the last three books (86; 103; 145). With these locations in mind,
the contribution of the parallels of the credo to the overall structure of
the Psalter will be analyzed. To these ends, the chapter will first outline
the current state of research on the Psalter as a whole literary unit, then
each of the parallels of the credo will be analyzed following the usual
diachronic-synchronic pattern.

SCHOLARLY ANALYSIS OF THE PSALTER

Traditionally, readers have approached the Psalter as a varied, haphazard
collection of psalms which contain no evidence of interconnection or a
broader literary pattern.[1] The Psalter itself, however, marks several sub-
sections within the larger collection. For example, Psalms 42–49 form a

---

1. Hermann Gunkel has bluntly remarked, "No internal ordering principle for the
individual psalms has been transmitted for the whole" (*Introduction to the Psalms*, 2).

"Korahite Collection" based upon superscriptions attributing the psalms "to Korah" and Psalms 42–83 form the "Elohistic Psalter" based upon common themes and the continued use of the divine name Elohim.[2] Between these collections, no full-fledged pattern is found in the overall structure of the Psalter as many psalms do not belong to a collection or two or more collections sometimes overlap.

Contemporary scholarship has moved toward analyzing the shape of the Psalter as a whole. This movement began with a modest proposal by Claus Westermann in 1962 that Psalms 1–119 formed the original Psalter.[3] Based upon the arrangement and concentration of different forms within the Psalter, Westermann argued that Psalms 1 and 119 were added late to the collection of Psalms 2–118 which moved the collection from a liturgical collection to a group to be studied.[4] This corpus was further divided between the Davidic (3–41) and Elohistic Psalter (42–83), which were encased by Royal Psalms (2, 89), and then Psalms of the Kingdom of YHWH (93–99).[5] Westermann's most lasting contributions are twofold—he sees an overall movement in the Psalter from individual lament to communal praise and a belief that the Royal Psalms were added at a later date when they would have had a secondary messianic theme.[6]

Following the lead of Westermann, Childs found some structural patterns within the Psalter.[7] Childs finds a strong royal theme within the Psalter based upon the reuse of older Royal Psalms. He sees, like Westermann, a shift in the Royal Psalms away from the historical David toward "a witness to the messianic hope which looked for the consummation of God's kingship through his Anointed One."[8] Toward this royal emphasis Childs sees the placement of Psalm 2 at the beginning of the Psalter along with the strategic locations of Psalms 72, 89 and 132 as

---

2. For a complete list of the different collections within the Psalter see DeClaissé-Walford, *Introduction to the Psalms*, 35–36.

3. Westermann, *Praise and Lament in the Psalms*, 250–58.

4. Ibid., 252–53.

5. Ibid., 254–55.

6. Ibid., 258.

7. Childs, *Introduction to the Old Testament*, 511–22.

8. Ibid., 517.

emphatic.[9] Childs also suggests that Psalm 1 serves as an introduction to the entire Psalter showing the collection to be something that should be meditated upon.[10] The importance of Childs' work is his clearer explication of the function of Royal Psalms and royal imagery and their importance for the shape of the Psalter.

Gerald Wilson, a student of Childs, published a dissertation that offers the most detailed proposal for the ordering of the Psalter.[11] In Wilson's view, the first three books of the Psalter function as a lament over the inadequacies of the human monarchy and the disappointment of the exile; this lament in the first three books is met with royal imagery and praise that YHWH is the eternal king who can be trusted in the last two books—Book IV is a return to Torah and Mosaic authority that asserts the reign of YHWH, before Book V praises YHWH's kingship in a multitude of heterogeneous ways.[12] Wilson's work ends with the strong affirmation, "Human 'princes' will wither and fade like grass, but the steadfast love of YHWH endures for ever."[13] He finds this overall theme by paying special attention to superscriptions, psalms at the seams between the five books and the overall theme of each book.

Wilson furthered his thesis with several important articles. We will examine two.[14] The first article further explicates the function of the Royal Psalms at the seams of the first three books of the Psalter. He shows that Psalm 2, which begins Book I, offers a positive evaluation of the Davidic covenant which continues through Psalm 72 and now asserts that, "David's assurance (Ps. 41) is now passed on to his descendents in this series of petitions in behalf of 'the king's son' (Ps. 72)."[15] Psalm 89, which concludes Book III, finds a dramatic change in the tone toward the monarchy as it laments the failure of the Davidic king.[16] Wilson sees within these three books a marked lament that first celebrates the

---

9. Ibid.

10. Ibid., 513.

11. Wilson, *The Editing of the Hebrew Psalter*. It should be noted that while Wilson did study with Childs, this dissertation was under the supervision of Robert Wilson.

12. Ibid., 209–28.

13. Ibid., 228.

14. Wilson, "The Use of Royal Psalms," 85–94; and Wilson, "Shaping the Psalter," 72–82.

15. Wilson, "The Use of Royal Psalms," 88–89.

16. Ibid., 91–92.

Davidic monarchy, and then laments its failure. He believes this lamentation shows the collection to be post-exilic as the community mourned the fall of the kingdom and the Davidic monarchy.

Wilson's second article looks for key terms and phrases that might provide a clue as to how Books IV–V were grafted onto the earlier collection of Books I–III. Based upon earlier work, he sees a "Royal Covenantal Frame" holding together Books I–III, while the final two books evidence the "concerns of wisdom."[17] In addition to these two frames, Wilson sees a "Final Wisdom Frame" in Psalms 1 and 145 that links the two larger collections together.[18] Wilson believes the place given to this "Final Wisdom Frame" gives more emphasis to its themes, than the earlier royal imagery. Wilson states, "In the final analysis, the shape of the canonical Psalter preserves a tense dialogue (or a dialogue in tension) between the royal covenantal hopes associated with the first two-thirds of the Psalter and the wisdom counsel to trust YHWH alone associated with the final third."[19] The Psalter, in its final shape, is a dramatic celebration of YHWH's reign in spite of the failure of the Davidic monarchy.

Wilson's work also has a strong diachronic component. Based upon collections of the Psalter found at Qumran, he has posited that by the first century BCE the first three books of the Psalter were relatively firmly established.[20] After a survey of evidence for the canonical arrangement of psalms found at Qumran, he posits a marked difference after Book III where "examples of variations [in order], practically non-existent in the first three books, increase markedly in Books Four and Five."[21] In a later article, Wilson argues for a first-century CE closing of the Psalter.[22] Wilson's argumentation focuses on the fixed nature of Psalms 1–89 at Qumran vis-à-vis the fluidity of the last two books.

Wilson's work stands as the bench mark for all current discussion on the shape and shaping of the Psalter. Many scholars have accepted

---

17. Wilson, "Shaping the Psalter," 80.

18. Ibid., 81.

19. Ibid., 81.

20. Wilson, *The Editing of the Hebrew Psalter*, 120–21.

21. Ibid., 121.

22. Wilson, "A First Century CE Date for the Closing for the Book of Psalms," 102–10.

and built upon his foundation.[23] The subsequent articles published after his dissertation have shored up the thesis of his dissertation. Not all have accepted his proposals, however. Norman Whybray takes issue with the understanding that the Psalter is a book.[24] He examines three areas which might prove fruitful for finding editorial linkage or overall thematic coherence within the Psalter—wisdom and torah material, eschatological reinterpretations and ritual sacrifice revisions. In each case, he finds the evidence lacking. He concludes that, "It is not possible to give a confident answer to the question whether the final redaction of the Psalter was undertaken in order to make it into a single, coherent book to be read privately."[25] He also believes it too long to be used in the cult. Whybray does find resonance with Wilson in the assertion that wisdom elements (such as the place of Psalm 1 or the inordinate length of Psalm 119) may give hermeneutical clues about how to read the Psalter; by wisdom elements, however, he does not see an emphasis on the reign of YHWH, but on meditation on the Torah.[26]

In spite of Whybray's detractions, others have found success building upon the foundation laid by Wilson. In 1997, Nancy deClaissé-Walford argued that the beginning psalms of each book are important in addition to the last.[27] The work of deClaissé-Walford reaffirms the work of Wilson, but also makes stronger diachronic statements about the shaping of the Psalter. She holds that ancient Israel's postexilic condition forced the community to re-imagine and shape the Psalter in a way that emphasized YHWH's kingship.[28] She states, "The postexilic community found a new structure for existence and identity by redefining 'nationhood' in the context of its culture in the ancient Near East. King, court, and temple were gone, but Israel survived."[29] This survival in spite of the

---

23. E.g., J. Clinton McCann sees the same general movement as Wilson, but argues that the themes of hope in Books IV–V are foreshadowed in Books I–III (McCann, "Books I–III and the Editorial Purpose of the Hebrew Psalter"). Marvin Tate sees several over-arching themes within the collections and looks for inter-psalm links (Tate, *Psalms 51–100*)

24. Whybray, *Reading the Psalter as a Book.*

25. Ibid., 123.

26. Ibid., 120–21.

27. DeClaissé-Walford, *Reading from the Beginning.*

28. Ibid., 121.

29. Ibid., 121–22.

loss of normative structures of identity is because the nation "appropriated and shaped its traditional and cultic material into a constitutive
document of identity, the Hebrew Scriptures. And the Psalter is a part of
that constitutive document."[30] Her work not only outlines the themes of
kingship in the Psalter, but also its sociological importance for sustaining
and centralizing the broken people.

J. Clinton McCann also sees kingship as an important motif in
the Psalter.[31] McCann sees Psalms 1 and 2 as a double introduction to
the Psalter—Psalm 1 holds that the collection should be taken up and
studied; Psalm 2 gives the "essential context of that instruction—the
Lord reigns!"[32] McCann, following Wilson, sees Book IV providing
the "theological heart" of the Psalter after the disappointment of Books
I–III.[33] Book IV, which is dominated by enthronement psalms, proclaim
YHWH's reign. The remainder of McCann's book is a sampling of psalms;
he continually returns to the idea of the reign of YHWH.

Two other proposals offer analyses based upon canonical readings of the Psalter. Walter Brueggemann suggests that the Psalter begins
with a call to obedience in Psalm 1 and culminates in praise in Psalm
150.[34] This call to obedience proposes that only those who are numbered
among the upright can sing/pray the psalms to follow.[35] With Psalm 150,
Brueggemann sees ancient Israel's most extreme and unqualified expression of praise. He believes this kind of extreme praise can only come as
a final statement after all other reasons have been given. "The Psalter, in
correspondence to Israel's life with God when lived faithfully, ends in
glad, unconditional praise: completely, and without embarrassment or
distraction, focused on God."[36] Between this call to obedience and unfettered praise, Brueggemann finds a movement within the Psalter that is
emblematic of ancient Israel's crisis of faith because of incongruities between lived experience and God's promised loving kindness. He believes

30. Ibid., 122.

31. McCann, *A Theological Introduction to the Book of the Psalms*.

32. Ibid., 41.

33. Ibid., 44.

34. Brueggemann, "Bounded by Obedience and Praise," 189–213.

35. Ibid., 191.

36. Ibid., 193.

Psalm 73 to embody this movement on two levels.[37] First, the psalm comes immediately after the postscript which announces that the "The prayers of David, son of Jesse, are ended" (72:20). This canonical break also sees a movement from a high concentration of lament psalms toward praise. Second, the structure of the psalm itself embodies the move from dutiful obedience to delightful praise. In summary, Brueggemann sees within the Psalter a pattern of faith fully embodied by ancient Israel.

John H. Walton offers a synopsis of the Psalter based upon the idea of a cantata.[38] Inspired by Wilson's work, Walton sees within the Psalter a loose, general history of ancient Israel from David's conflict with Saul (Book I), David's reign (Book II), Assyrian Crisis (Book III), Introspection about Destruction of the Temple and Exile (Book IV) and Praise/Reflection on Return and New Era (Book V).[39] Throughout the Psalter, Walton pays special attention to historical clues within psalms and superscriptions. For example, he sees a transition from David's monarchy to Solomon's rule expressed in Psalms 71–72 which see David as old and gray (71:18), and then gives David's blessing on Solomon (72:15–17).[40] Walton's organization works well overall, but several significant historical events are not recorded in the Psalter's retelling of the story. For example, he finds no psalm to match the Davidic covenant of 2 Samuel 7 and there is no mention of the exile/destruction of Jerusalem in its chronological place within the Psalter, only a backwards introspection on these events. Psalm 137, the most explicit reference to the actual exile/Destruction of Jerusalem, comes in Book V which is devoted to praise centered on the return to the land.

In summary, I find the following conclusions most relevant to our study. First, the Psalter evidences an editorial arrangement which laments the demise of the human Davidic monarchy, and then celebrates the reign of YHWH over the cosmos. This movement evidences some foreshadowing in the early books, but a definite move from lament to praise can be found. The credo appears in psalms which celebrate YHWH's reign. Second, central to this argument are Royal Psalms and

---

37. Ibid., 204–5. See also Brueggemann and Miller, "Psalm 73 as a Canonical Marker," 45–56. McCann also argues that Psalm 73 provides a short theological snapshot of the faith expressed in the Psalter ("Psalm 73," 247–57).

38. Walton, "Psalms: A Cantata about the Davidic Covenant," 21–31.

39. Ibid., 24.

40. Ibid., 26–27.

psalms at the "seams" between the books. While the credo only occurs in one seam psalm (Psalm 145), the two other major occurrences are near the end of Books III (Psalm 86) and IV (Psalm 103). Third, the Psalter also evidences a movement from dutiful obedience to exuberant praise. The credo, and its components which highlight YHWH's covenantal attributes, form the basis for much of the exuberant praise. Last, the Psalter is one of the last canonical collections to find its final form. The expressions of the credo found within the Psalter evidence some of the most dramatic reinterpretations of any of the canonical expressions. These dramatic changes may be due to their late addition to the canon.

The remaining pages in this chapter will explore the appearances of the credo within the Psalter and its contribution to the Psalter's canonical shape. Each occurrence will be examined in canonical order, with an examination of diachronic issues first, then a consideration of its synchronic location.

PSALM 86

The first canonical appearance of the credo in the Psalter comes in Psalm 86. In this lament, the psalmist beckons for YHWH to intercede and "hear," "guard," "have mercy" and "bring joy" (86:1–4). The psalmist uses the credo as an expression of the faithfulness of YHWH's character and the reason why YHWH should come to the aid of this worshipper. The lament ends with assurance that God will indeed act on behalf of the one offering the lament.

Diachronic Issues

It is difficult to find an exact date for the composition of Psalm 86. The psalm and its superscription are without any clear historical markers. Mitchell Dahood believes the text originated with an ancient Israelite king because of the use of "your servant" (86:4, 5, 8, 9, 12, 15) which he believes to be a title spoken by a vassal to the suzerain and by the large scale effects of YHWH's intervention described in 86:9.[41] J. H. Eaton also dates the psalm to the time of the monarchy based upon the servant theme, nature of the enemies and the extent of God's rule which he sees as char-

41. Dahood, *Psalms II*, 292.

acteristic of psalms of that era.[42] Eaton also believes the psalm to be royal, but not necessarily from David.[43] Both Dahood and Eaton are correct in seeing that the psalm has royal imagery, but the presence of this imagery does not necessary indicate a royal origin. A later author could have used the servant imagery to describe the vassal/suzerain relationship between YHWH, the great king, and the worshiper. As will be discussed below, this imagery could certainly be early, without the entire psalm being early.

On the other hand, most scholars see the text as a late postexilic composition. Frank L. Hossfeld and Erich Zenger find a late date based upon the use of the terms "needy and poor" (86:1), "faithful" (86:2), and "your servant" (86:2, 4, 16) juxtaposed with the groups that seek to derail the faithfulness of the servant.[44] Hossfeld and Zenger later admit, however, that "at present we cannot go beyond speculation."[45]

A better explanation for a late date for the writing of Psalm 86 comes in its composition. The psalm contains parallels with several works other than Exod 34:6–7. Consider the following large parallels with other psalms.[46] In 86:1b, the psalmist proclaims that "I am afflicted and needy" which is directly paralleled in Ps 40:17. In 86:11, we have a petition, "YHWH, teach me your way," a quotation of 27:11. 86:14 is an indirect quotation of Ps 54:3. The original states, "For the arrogant have risen against me and violent ones are seeking my life; they have not placed God before them." Psalm 86 slightly alters the original: "O God, the arrogant men have risen against me and a gathering of violent ones seek my life; and they have not set you before them" (86:14).

42. Eaton, *Psalms*, 212.

43. Ibid.

44. Hossfeld and Zenger, *Psalms 2*, 371.

45. Ibid., 371.

46. Many others have seen connections with other texts. Pigott, "God of Compassion and Mercy," 169, offers the most extensive list: Ps 86:1a parallels Pss 17:6, 31:2, 71:2; Ps 86:1b parallels Pss 40:17, 70:5; Ps 86:2a parallels Pss 4:3, 25:20; Ps 86:2b parallels Pss 25:2, 31:14, 56:4; Ps 86:3a parallels Pss 4:1, 57:1; Ps 86:4b parallels Pss 25:1, 143:8; Ps 86:5a parallels Pss 25:8, 130:4; Ps 86:5b parallels Exod 34:6, Neh 9:17, Pss 103:8, 145:8, Joel 2:13, Jon 4:2; Ps 86:6 parallels Ps 55:1; Ps 86:7a parallels Pss 50:15, 77:2; Ps 86:7b parallels Ps 17:6; Ps 86:8a parallels Exod 15:11, 2 Sam 7:22, 1 Kgs 8:23; Ps 89:6 parallels Jer 10:6; Ps 86:9a parallels Pss 22:27, 66:4, Isa 66:23; Ps 86:10a parallels Pss 72:18, 77:14, 136:4, Ps 86:11a parallels Ps 25:5; Ps 86:12a parallels Ps 111:1; Ps 86:13b parallels Ps 30:3; Ps 86:14a parallels Ps 54:3; Ps 86:15 parallels Exod 34:6; Ps 86:16a parallels Pss 25:16; Ps 86:16bc parallels Ps 116:16; Ps 86:17a parallels Ps 119:122; Ps 86:17b parallels Ps 112:10.

This composite nature along with the reliance on Exod 34:6–7 and the narrative of Exodus 32–34 may point to a later date for the text. Marvin Tate believes the text is from "learned scribal circles of the pious" and thus dates it during the late postexilic period.[47] The great number of textual connections shows that the author of the psalm was extremely fluent in the language of biblical texts. This fluency may be a mark of both a later date and a highly literate person who had texts at his or her disposal. Many others have reached the same conclusion and dated the text late.[48]

Even with the composite nature of the text, it is difficult to date the text more precisely than postexilic, but several diachronic statements can be made. First, the overall positive nature of the parallel shows that a postexilic community represented by Psalm 86 moved away from exclusivist claims, toward universal affirmations of YHWH's compassionate rule over all the nations. For the first time, the credo is used to show that YHWH will extend his compassion to all the nations. Second, the late diachronic dating of this parallel coupled with its brevity and exclusive focus on the merciful characteristics of YHWH provide evidence that the credo did not grow from an early version which only included Exod 34:6 to include 34:7 only after the exile.[49] This late parallel only quotes the first portions of the credo.

Participation in Exodus 34:6–7

This appearance of the credo contains the fullest expression of Exod 34:6–7 in the *Kethuvim*. The psalm actually contains two allusions to the credo. In 86:5, the psalmist praises YHWH because God is "great in loving kindness" (רַב־חֶסֶד) and extends it to all who call on him. This appearance of the phrase רַב־חֶסֶד is the only time in the Hebrew Bible that is not directly connected with a quotation of the credo. This brief allusion also serves as the crescendo in a series of attributes in 86:5 which

---

47. Tate, *Psalms 51–100*, 380.

48. See Anderson, *Psalms 73–150*, 614; Kraus, *Psalms 60–150*, 181; Oesterley, *The Psalms*, 387.

49. For those that argue for an expansion of the credo, see Perlitt, *Bundestheologie im Alten Testament*, 214; Sakenfeld, *The Meaning of Hesed in the Hebrew Bible*, 130–31; Hermann Spieckermann, "'Barmherzig und gnädig ist der Herr . . . ,'" 3.

moves from "good," to "forgiving," and finally "great in loving kindness."[50] With the allusion, the psalmist foreshadows the longer quotation that comes later in the prayer. A second allusion comes in 86:13 as the psalmist proclaims that YHWH's loving kindness is great toward the poet. The poet specifically cites his salvation from the deepest parts of Sheol as an example of God's loving kindness in action.

The major quotation of the credo comes in 86:15. The psalmist believes that the reason why YHWH should help is because, "You are the Lord, gracious and compassionate, slow to anger and great in loving kindness and faithfulness." The first noticeable change is that "you are Lord" (וְאַתָּה אֲדֹנָי) replaces the double name (יְהוָה יְהוָה). The change emphasizes the reign of YHWH and continues the vassal/lord imagery from earlier in the poem.[51] With this exception, the only other change is that the psalmist ended the quotation after the first three sections of the credo are rehearsed. The poet does not give any of the attributes of Exod 34:7. Only YHWH's merciful attributes are given.

The inclusion of YHWH's gracious and compassionate nature, greatness in loving kindness, and faithfulness both motivates God to act and reminds the psalmist of the past actions of YHWH. Hossfeld and Zenger see within the quotation a recollection of all of YHWH's previous salvific works from the Exodus until the time of the poet.[52] The poet reminds YHWH of past acts of salvation for the community to elicit salvation for the individual. The recollection of the past salvation is followed by four imperatives in 86:16–17 summoning YHWH to act—"turn" (פָּנָה), "be gracious" (חָנַן), "give strength" (נָתַן־עֹז), and "save" (יָשַׁע). It is clear that the poet imagines the affirmation of these attributes as having a positive effect on YHWH's actions.

The only surprising attribute given is YHWH's slowness to anger. In no place has the psalmist admitted guilt. Rather, this poet is "poor and needy" (86:1), is devoted to YHWH (86:2) and lifts up his soul to God (86:4). In fact, the psalmist even takes up a variant (חָסִיד-"pious") of the thrice used attribute of YHWH's "loving kindness" (חֶסֶד) as a self description. The closest that the palmist comes to an admission of guilt is the promise to "walk in your truth" and "fear your name" in 86:11.

---

50. Hossfeld and Zenger, *Psalms 2*, 372.

51. For more about vassal/lord imagery, see Dahood, *Psalms II*, 293.

52. Hossfeld and Zenger, *Psalms 2*, 375.

Neither of those statements assumes a change for the future; both could simply be an affirmation that the poet plans to continue current activities. Nevertheless, the psalmist's inclusion of this attribute is surprising considering that nothing has been mentioned that might provoke YHWH's anger.

Most of the excluded attributes can also be explained by context. First, the wrathful attributes were all excised because the psalmist sought YHWH's mercy. The inclusion of these characteristics would not have helped the poet's argument. Second, the poet omits YHWH's extension of loving kindness "to thousands" because he does not seek mercy for thousands, but simply for himself.[53] This psalm takes the covenantal credo, which to this point has been used in reference to ancient Israel as a corporate body, and uses it to marshal YHWH's mercy for deliverance in private misfortune. Third, the psalmist also redacts the "taking away iniquity, transgression and sin." Again, I believe this redaction relates to the reason that caused the exclusion of wrathful attributes; the poet does not seek forgiveness, but mercy and loving kindness.[54]

Participation in the Larger Narrative

Psalm 86 is a lament and is structured as such. Several petitions mark the psalm's structure. These petitions use imperatives to move YHWH to act on behalf of the poet (86:1–4, 6, 16, 17). As usual for the Lament Psalms, the prayer ends on a hopeful note with praise as the psalmist proclaims, "For you are YHWH; you have helped and comforted me" (Psalm 86:17). The prayer is slightly unusual in that it does not simply move from plea to praise as do other laments (cf. Psalms 10; 13). The psalm moves from petition (1–7) to praise (8–13) and back to petition and praise in the final section (14–17).[55]

A second structure also exists in the psalm. Bellinger sees a structure which centers around doxologies arranged in a "stair-step parallelism" in

53. Pigott, "God of Compassion and Mercy," 173.

54. Pigott believes that this phrase was left out because the psalmist acknowledged the forgiving nature of God in 86:5 with the use of סלּח (ibid., 174). This explanation does not match the style of this psalmist who has three times spoken of YHWH's loving kindness.

55. Others also divide the psalm in this way. See Dahood, *Psalms II*, 292; Tate, *Psalms 51–100*, 380–81; Pigott, "God of Compassion," 171–72; and Hossfeld and Zenger, *Psalms 2*, 369–70.

86:5, 10, 15.[56] I would add 86:13 as part of this parallelism. As noted above, 86:5 is a doxology which centers on an allusion of the credo which begins with the particle יִכּ, "because of." Again in 86:10, the particle introduces the doxology which praises YHWH's greatness and doing of marvelous deeds. The particle comes a third time in 86:13 which again praises YHWH's loving kindness and deliverance from the lowest parts of Sheol.

The last doxology of the poem comes with the quotation of the credo in 86:15. Although this doxology is not introduced by a יִכּ, it is obviously a doxology. The יִכּ is replaced with אַתָּה "you." Brueggemann believes that the use of the independent pronoun rather than a pronominal suffix suggests that it is an "independent element used to make a strong expression."[57] The poet moves away from the particle to the more emphatic personal pronoun to give special emphasis to this doxology. He piles up the positive attributes to a degree unmatched in this psalm.

The doxology based upon the credo comes as the climax of the final section in 86:15. Unlike the first part of the poem which moved from petition to praise, this section brackets the petition with praise. The section begins with a description of the problem ("the arrogant are attacking me"—86:14) which is juxtaposed by the dramatic doxology praising YHWH's mercy and compassion (86:15). This doxology is followed by the extended series of imperatives aimed at YHWH ("turn," "grant," "save," "give"—86:16–17a). The final two phrases announce that the enemies will see YHWH's action and be put to shame (86:17b).

I believe that the inverse order of the plea and praise in this section gives added emphasis and is emblematic of the whole psalm. The move from praise to plea shows that the psalmist's hopes for deliverance do not rest in her own חֶסֶד, but in the character of YHWH. The intensity of the psalm also reaches a crescendo with the heightened doxology quickly followed by the string of imperatives. The psalmist uses the extended doxology to gain YHWH's attention, as did Moses in Numbers 14, then quickly follows with the four imperatives imploring God to act. The concentration of positive attributes and imperatives show this final section to be climactic.

---

56. Bellinger, *Psalms*, 40. Bellinger defines "stair-step parallelism" as the continuation and furtherance of the thought of the first line by the second line (13).

57. Brueggemann, *The Message of the Psalms*, 62.

In the larger narrative, Psalm 86 stands as the only Davidic Psalm in Book III. This peculiarity is intensified by the fact that Psalm 86 breaks a string of Korahite Psalms which run from Psalms 84–88. Furthermore, Psalm 89 is connected to the Korahite collection by use of the superscription "a maskil of . . . the Ezrahite"(. . . הָאֶזְרָחִי מַשְׂכִּיל) in both Psalm 88 and 89.[58]

Considering these connections, Psalm 86 participates in the lament over the Davidic monarchy that comes in Book III in three ways. First, the poem emphasizes YHWH's covenantal relationship with the other nations as it proclaims that all of the nations will come to bow down before YHWH and bring glory (86:9). Hossfeld and Zenger see connections with Psalm 87 in that the "nations" of Psalm 86 will soon be the inhabitants of Zion.[59] Tate also sees a connection between the two psalms suggesting that Psalm 87's location gives emphasis to the multinational claims of Psalm 86.[60] Psalm 87 certainly extends and solidifies the prediction of Psalm 86 from simply "the nations" (86:9) to an actual list of the nations present which includes Rahab, Babylon, Philistia, Tyre and Cush (87:4). All of these nations will have citizenship in Zion. The merciful attributes of YHWH given in 86:15 are freely and fully offered to the other nations. The shape of the Psalter assumes the extension of these attributes to the other nations and YHWH's *de facto* reign over all the earth, as opposed to the localized reign of David.

Second, this Davidic psalm gives the Korahite collection an infusion of hope based on YHWH's rule. Hossfeld and Zenger find a large lament in the structure of the collection with Pss 84:1–85:8 forming the lament/petition and Pss 85:9–14; 87:1–7 contributing the divine response.[61] On the other hand, Psalms 84 and 85 are laments, but both contain positive elements that could be taken as an indication that the poet has already heard the salvation oracle or divine response (84:10–12; 85:8–13). It is more plausible to read Psalms 86 and 87 as foreshadowing the hope that will be announced in Books IV–V as suggested by McCann.[62] The

58. Wilson, *The Editing of the Hebrew Psalter*, 157.

59. Hossfeld and Zenger, *Psalms 2*, 376.

60. Tate, *Psalms 51–100*, 380.

61. Hossfeld and Zenger, *Psalms 2*, 387.

62. Although McCann finds foreshadowing in the first psalm of each book, his suggestion shows that each book is not monolithic, but already hints at the wonder of YHWH's reign ("Books I–III and the Editorial Purpose of the Hebrew Psalter," 104).

exuberance of Psalms 86 and 87, which centers on the opening of the merciful attributes of the credo freely to the other nations, tempers the darkness of Psalm 88 and then the lament over the broken Davidic covenant in Psalm 89. The Psalter gives the reader clues to the outcome of this broken covenant with a juxtaposition of the reign of YHWH and reign of the Davidic kings. The attributes of the credo play an important role in defining the character of the reign of YHWH.

Third, Psalm 86 is also linked to Books I–II by the Davidic superscription.[63] As was noted above, it is the only psalm in Book III which carries the Davidic superscription, which is surprising considering the large collections of Davidic psalms in the first two books (Pss 3–41; 51–72). This scarcity makes the Davidic superscription of Psalm 86 even more pronounced. Furthermore, the content of the psalm is an admission by David that the lofty expectations of the earthly king as expressed in Psalm 72, the final Davidic psalm, have gone unmet. This prayer of David holds that YHWH is merciful and compassionate and does goodness. The rule of the earthly king is not even mentioned.

Our examination of the appearance of the credo in Psalm 86 leaves us with five summary statements:

1. The dramatic reshaping of the credo toward the merciful attributes of YHWH shows a theological shift in a late postexilic community toward a reliance on God's grace and mercy as the source of hope for the community.

2. The credo relies exclusively on the merciful characteristics of YHWH.

3. The attributes of the credo provide a structure for the doxologies of Psalm 86.

4. Psalm 86 infuses the final psalms of Book III, that center on the failure of the Davidic monarchy, with a dramatic hope based upon the reign of YHWH.

5. Psalms 86–87 when joined canonically with Psalms 88–89 make it clear that YHWH's reign is not to be seen in the monarchy.

---

63. Wilson, "Shaping the Psalter," 78.

PSALM 103

Psalm 103 uses the credo as an affirmation of the overwhelmingly positive character of YHWH's reign. The psalm is a thanksgiving from a person who has personally experienced YHWH's mercy after having been brought back from the brink of death (103:4), even though the poet did not deserve it (103:10). The attributes of the credo appear throughout the poem to describe God as the poet continually returns to YHWH's merciful qualities for description. The poet offers a dramatic portrait whereby "the powers of the other world and all the works of creation render homage" to this divine king.[64]

Diachronic Issues

Psalm 103 most likely originated in the postexilic period. Most commentators are hesitant to offer a more specific date because the text offers no concrete historical clues. Commentators who date the text to the postexilic period look to two clues to find a tentative date. First, the psalm quotes from the latter portions of Isaiah, texts which are supposed to have originated late during the exile or after. The first quotation expresses praise over the fact that YHWH's anger does not last forever (Isa 57:16→Ps 103:9). The second quotation uses the metaphor of the transitory nature of grass and flowers to describe the human condition of mortality (Isa 40:6–7→Ps 103:15–16). Second, the poet used an Aramaic suffix (כִי) four times in Ps 103:3–5.

   Based upon these factors, Kraus gives the text a late postexilic date.[65] He suggests that the general nature of its praises and thanksgivings show it to be a "formulary used in the sanctuary" in which "numerous petitioners with a variety of distresses, problems, and afflictions could find a place and so appear before God."[66] Moses Buttenwieser finds a specific historical date for the Psalm—332/331 BCE when Alexander the Great gave to Judea renewed privileges which helped the nation recover from the harm of Artaxerxes III Ochus.[67] He finds this date because of a loose connection with Job (Job 14:1–2), which he takes to be written after 400.

---

64. Kraus, *Psalms 60–150*, 294.

65. Ibid., 290.

66. Ibid.

67. Buttenwieser, *The Psalms*, 681–82.

He then finds within almost every line a connection to Alexander the Great!

Not all commentators have been as eager as Kraus or as chronologically specific as Buttenwieser. Michael Dahood believes the text to be earlier than postexilic.[68] He argues that the Aramaic suffixes may be a Canaanite archaism and that Isaiah 40 and 57 and Psalm 103 may have borrowed from a common source.[69] Pigott is hesitant to cite a date simply because of the absence of any historical markers.[70] Most of these interpreters simply believe that the evidence is too sparse to make a firm commitment to date the text.

In my opinion, the firmest conclusion is that the psalm's final shape is a product of the postexilic period. Buttenwieser's dating is far too precise to be probable. The quotations from the latter parts of Isaiah point to a later date. Furthermore, the Aramaic suffixes could also come from this time.[71] While Dahood's criticism is relevant, it causes as many problems as it helps. The creation of a hypothetical source for both Psalm 103 and Isaiah is not a neat and tidy answer. For these reasons, the most plausible scenario is that the psalm is late, not early.

Assuming that the final shape of the psalm is postexilic, then the parallel of the credo functions as support for the announcement of the supremacy of YHWH's rule. The postexilic nation would have likely been stricken with competing foreign and domestic rulers staking their claim over Yehud. This psalm heralds the fact that YHWH's rule is supreme and as such is the only rule which should be given priority. The temporal, transient kingdoms which are vying for the loyalties of Yehud should not be trusted. This psalm proclaims that a reliance on YHWH's kingship is the only hope of stability for the people.

Participation in Exodus 34:6–7

The parallel of the credo comes in Ps 103:8. This version of the credo contains four connections to the original—"YHWH," "compassionate and gracious," "slow to anger," and "great in loving kindness." As can

---

68. Dahood, *Psalms III*, 103.

69. Ibid., 103.

70. Pigott, "God of Compassion and Mercy," 176.

71. See Leslie C. Allen, who also believes that מלכות of 103:20 could also be an Aramaism (*Psalms 101–150*, 28).

be seen immediately, the text focuses completely on the merciful attributes of YHWH as do the other parallels in the Psalter. The psalm is a rehearsal of the wonderful characteristics of YHWH's reign so the quotation certainly fits the context. The psalmist's use of the credo emphasizes the overwhelmingly positive nature of YHWH's reign. For the psalmist, this reign is characterized by God's ability to forgive. At least four times, the psalm makes a direct reference to YHWH's ability to save (103:3, 9, 12, 13). N. H. Parker summarizes the conclusions of the poet which are based upon the credo, God "is not an arbitrary, relentless administrator of justice meting out to men the precise retribution appropriate to their misdeeds."[72]

The first connection with the original comes with the use of the divine name YHWH. The psalm is a tribute to YHWH and the divine name occurs eleven times in twenty-two verses. This high concentration shows that YHWH is the subject of the poet's praise. The second connection comes with the recitation of YHWH's "compassionate and gracious" nature. This combination of attributes summarizes the psalmist's feelings about YHWH. The root רחם occurs two other times (103:13) and is used to compare a parent's compassion to the compassion of YHWH. Along with the forgiveness theme of the psalm, this attribute holds that God's compassion is marked by a caring that prevails over anger.[73] YHWH's gracious nature emphasizes God's willingness to offer pardon.

The third and fourth connections come with the affirmation that YHWH is "slow to anger" and "great in loving kindness." This combination expresses the sentiments of forgiveness in both positive and negative ways. The psalm begins with a list of the benefits of a relationship with this God who is great in loving kindness (103:1–5), but who also recognizes that the human covenant partner is weak and mortal (103:10, 12, 13, 15). This attribute shows that God does not demand the same level of covenantal action as is offered. This disparity is allowed because of YHWH's slowness to anger. Brueggemann believes that this piling on of merciful attributes shows the reader that "Yahweh shatters all expectations and does not treat us as we might anticipate."[74]

The parallel omits all of the wrathful attributes of Exod 34:7 and some of the merciful attributes of Exod 34:6. The exclusion of wrath-

---

72. Parker, "Psalm 103," 192.

73. Mays, *Psalms*, 328.

74. Brueggemann, *Message of the Psalms*, 160.

ful attributes at first seems quite natural in this psalm which centers on YHWH's forgiveness, but the poet gives many other clues towards YHWH's wrathful nature. The poet repeatedly mentions the conditional nature of YHWH's forgiveness—the heights of the heavens above the earth give a clue to the degree of God's love for "those who fear him" (103:11); YHWH has compassion on "those who fear him" (103:13); God's loving kindness is extended to "those who fear him" (103:17); covenant obedience must precede all who want God's loving kindness (103:18). Even if the psalmist does not quote the wrathful attributes of Exod 34:7, those qualities are present in the poem. The poet also excluded "taking away iniquity, rebellion and sin." The poet does hint at this characteristic with the poetic reinterpretation that YHWH will not treat us as our sins deserve or repay according to our iniquities (103:10). This exclusion is made even more baffling as a full quotation of these attributes would have furthered the poet's emphasis on God's forgiveness.

In fact, the tension of the full credo would have matched the tension evident in the psalm. McCann sees the tension between justice and mercy for the God who "both wills and demands justice and righteousness and yet who loves and is committed to relationships with sinful people."[75] McCann thinks that this tension led the psalmist to quote from the credo.[76] McCann's judgment requires the reader to supply extra information which is not included in the text. Rather the psalmist subverts this tension by only quoting the merciful attributes of YHWH. This reading of the credo moves away from the tension toward an emphasis on YHWH's mercy. Westermann sees the psalm as an assertion of "the incomprehensible excess of God's goodness."[77] The psalmist distorted the balance of the original credo to match the emphasis on God's goodness in this psalm.

Participation in the Larger Context

This section will argue that the parallel to the credo plays a significant role in Psalm 103 and that Psalm 103 plays a significant role in the ending of Book IV. The credo provides a framework for the psalm. The prayer is not

75. McCann, "Psalms," 1092.

76. Ibid.

77. Westermann, *Elements of Old Testament Theology*, 139.

easily divided into sections.[78] The most appealing analysis comes from
Timothy Willis who divides the text into five strophes.[79] Echoes of the
credo appear in four of Willis' five strophes. The first strophe (103:1–5)
is a list of reasons why the psalmist's soul should bless YHWH. Two of
the five reasons given are connected to the imagery of the credo—God
forgives all our iniquity and crowns with loving kindness and mercy. The
second strophe (103:6–10) is an extended account of YHWH's forgiving nature. This strophe contains the actual parallel to the credo and the
echo mentioned above in 103:10. Strophe III (103:11–14) contains three
metaphors that describe YHWH's forgiveness. The second line of each
metaphor contains an echo—YHWH's loving kindness (חֶסֶד) is great
to the same degree that the heavens are above the earth; our transgressions (פֶּשַׁע) are removed as far as the East is from the West; and God
has mercy (רַחַם) on us like a parent has on a child. The fourth strophe
(103:15–19) contrasts the brevity of human life with the eternality of
God's existence. YHWH's infinite existence finds concrete expression in
the extension of loving kindness to each generation.

The attributes of YHWH give depth to the thanksgiving that the
poet offers. The text of the psalm is an extended celebration of the merciful God who rescues from the pit. Mays believes the psalm to be a proclamation that, "The LORD's steadfast love . . . is so abounding that it fills all
time and space."[80] Allen sees significance in the fact that "the theological
motif that dominates the psalm is Yahweh's חֶסֶד."[81] Even Buttenweiser,
who focuses mainly on diachronic issues, holds that YHWH's חֶסֶד "is the
central thought of the psalm, toward which all that precedes converges."[82]
The psalmist connects YHWH's loving kindness with actions both past
and present. In the past, YHWH has made known the divine ways to

78. Some divide the psalm into three sections (Allen, *Psalms 101–150*, 19–21);
some divide it into five sections (Kidner, *Psalms 73–150*, 363–67); some divide the
psalm into six sections (Westermann, *The Living Psalms*, 238); some divide the psalm
into nine sections (Briggs, *A Critical and Exegetical Commentary on the Book of
Psalms*, 324–27).

79. Willis, "'So Great is His Steadfast Love,'" 525–37. Willis' analysis is based upon
the rhetorical features of the text. His work not only helps to divide the psalm into
sections, but it also helps to illuminate the argumentation of the psalm.

80. Mays, *Psalms*, 328.

81. Allen, *Psalms 101–150*, 28.

82. Buttenweiser, *The Psalms*, 683.

Moses and the people of ancient Israel (103:7); currently, YHWH's throne is established in heaven and rules over all (103:19). The ending of the psalm emphasizes this universal rule with the quadruple imperatival summons (ברכו) for all the angels, all the heavenly warriors, all of the works of YHWH and even the psalmist's soul to "bless YHWH." McCann sees this last imperative as a self-admonition to "put oneself in tune with the whole cosmic order by acknowledging God's reign and by joining all beings in conforming to God's word and will."[83]

This universal expansion of YHWH's rule is also emphasized in the surrounding psalms that end Book IV. According to Wilson's schema for understanding the Psalter, Book IV emphasizes Mosaic themes and Torah piety. Wilson has shown that Psalms 105–106 along with Psalms 90–92 form a Mosaic frame for Book IV.[84] The last two psalms of Book IV (105–106) are both recollections of YHWH's past goodness to ancient Israel. I contend that Psalms 103–104 also form a pair. The two are connected by three points. First, both psalms begin and end with the command for the psalmist's soul to "bless God" (103:1, 22; 104:1, 35). These two psalms are the only two in Book IV to either begin or end in this way, further solidifying the connection. Second, both Psalms 103 and 104 use creation imagery to express their perspectives. Third, both psalms are expressions of God's reign over creation (103:19–21; 104:1–4). Mays sees the connection in that both offer variations on the same theme, "Together the pair [of psalms] praise the Lord as the savior who forgives and creator who provides."[85] In sum, Pss 103–104 are connected by both content and framing devices.

This couplet (Psalms 103–104) is also connected to the last two psalms of Book IV despite their apparent differences. All four begin with imperatives admonishing the reader to "praise" or "bless" YHWH. These are the only four psalms to begin this way in Book IV. The couplet of Psalms 103–104 praises YHWH as the divine king who reigns over all creation with compassion (Psalm 103) and with wisdom (Psalm 104). The second couplet (Psalms 105–106) praises YHWH as ancient Israel's covenant partner. These last two psalms of Book IV celebrate God's concrete acts of compassion and loving kindness to ancient Israel. The two

83. McCann, "Psalms," 1093.
84. Wilson, "Shaping the Psalter," 75–76.
85. Mays, *Psalms*, 331.

couplets are also connected by common terms. Psalm 103 uses the term "Moses" in parallel with and synonymously with the covenant people of ancient Israel (103:7) which looks forward to Psalm 106. This mention of Moses and ancient Israel comes immediately before the occurrence of the credo in Psalm 103—the psalmist mentions YHWH's ways and deeds, then speaks of God's forgiveness and compassion by using the credo. Psalm 106 is an extended rehearsal of God's miracles among the Moses generation of the Exodus. The poet of Psalm 106 also looks backward to Psalm 103 with the opening refrain, "Give thanks to YHWH who is good and whose loving kindness endures forever" (106:1). Several other times the psalmist refers to the past mighty acts of God as "loving kindness" (106:7, 45).

In sum, Psalm 103 and the credo play an important role in the final four psalms of Book IV. As Wilson has shown, the defining themes of Book IV are Moses and Torah fidelity. Psalms 105–106 emphasize these themes. The placement of Psalm 103 and its emphasis on YHWH's universal reign before Psalms 105–106 foreshadow the universal reign of YHWH that will dominate Book V. Also, the connection to Moses and ancient Israel gives clues to the reader that the scope of YHWH's reign will soon widen beyond the bounds of the covenant nation.

After the analysis of the credo in Psalm 103, there are four summary statements to be made:

1. The psalm functioned as a call to the people of the postexilic period to rely on the kingship of YHWH, rather than trust in the transitory earthly kings.

2. The parallel of the credo only rehearses YHWH's mercy and compassion, completely omitting wrathful characteristics.

3. The imagery of the credo permeates the psalm, especially YHWH's loving kindness over those things.

4. The psalm forms an integral part of the four psalms that end Book IV with a symphony of praises for different aspects of YHWH's character and past actions.

PSALM 145

The credo makes its final canonical appearance in the Psalter in Psalm 145. Psalm 145 ends Book V with an extended praise centering on God the King. The credo comes in 145:8 as a marker of the reign of YHWH. This psalm ends Book V with a recitation of the wonderful characteristics of YHWH's reign, and the attributes of the credo play an integral role in the theology of YHWH's reign.

Diachronic Issues

Most early interpreters held that Psalm 145 played a role in the annual enthronement festival because of its repeated affirmations of YHWH's reign. Werner Schmidt argues that the resounding theme of the everlasting reign of YHWH would have been particularly suited for the festival.[86] Recent interpreters, however, generally agree that Psalm 145 is a postexilic psalm.[87] Buttenweiser dates it later simply because of its "broad universalism."[88] Allen marshals more evidence for a postexilic date.[89] He again cites the use of the Aramaic ending of מלכות and the parallels with Psalms 103 and 111, which are also postexilic.[90] These features of Aramaic terms and intratextuality may show that the final form is late, but diachronic assertions should be tentative.

Much like Psalms 86 and 103, the psalmist uses the credo to describe the reign of YHWH as one that is governed by God's gracious and compassionate nature. For its postexilic audience, this reign is juxtaposed to the transitory reign of the rulers of the Persian and Greek empires. The psalm is an affirmation that YHWH's reign should be trusted because it is an "everlasting kingdom" and one which will endure "from generation to generation" (145:13). The psalmist used the old tradition of the credo as a rallying point for the nation under extreme duress from external political forces.

---

86. Schmidt, *Königtum Gottes in Ugarit und Israel*, 44.

87. See Dahood, who does not opt for an earlier period than postexilic, but who believes that "Neither content nor style afford a solid basis for determining the date of composition" (*Psalms III*, 336).

88 Buttenweiser, *The Psalms*, 849. Buttenweiser judges, without giving any evidence or further comment, that "Poetically the hymn is worthless. It appears to be a product of the time of literary decadence" (849).

89 Allen, *Psalms 101–150*, 371. See also Oesterley, who considers the psalm "One of the latest in the Psalter" (*The Psalms*, 572).

90 Allen, *Psalms 101–150*, 371. For more about the connection of Psalm 145 with other psalms see Holm-Nielson, "The Importance of Late Jewish Psalmody," 14–16.

Participation in Exodus 34:6–7

The parallel in the credo comes in Ps 145:8 and has four different connections with the original. The psalmist exclaims that "YHWH" is "gracious and compassionate," "slow to anger," and "great in loving kindness." This parallel of the credo is an almost exact replication of the parallel in Psalm 103. The only difference comes in the fact that Psalm 145 reverses the order of the normal "compassionate and gracious." The connection between the two parallels could be explained in that both psalms are declarations of YHWH's kingship over the universe. This connection can also be seen in the parallel in Psalm 86 which only adds "faithfulness" to the attributes listed in Psalms 103 and 145.

Psalm 145 is an acrostic. The inversion of "compassionate and gracious" most likely resulted because the poet used the credo in the ח line and thus placed חַנּוּן before רַחוּם. This reversal also occurs in the ח lines of Psalms 111 and 112.[91] Pigott believes that the inverse phrasing of gracious and compassionate may have been a common phrase used for the ח line in the same way that contemporary English commonly uses "x-ray" for the letter X or "zebra" for the letter Z in English acrostics.[92] The parallels of the credo in Jonah and Joel also inverse the order of the attributes, but are not located in an acrostic.

As with Psalm 103, the poet of Psalm 145 connects the universal reign of YHWH only with the gracious and compassionate nature of YHWH, and not with the wrathful, punishing God of Exod 34:7. Pigott believes that the wrathful attributes may have been excised because they did not fit into the next line of the acrostic.[93] She offers an interesting, but unsupported hypothesis regarding the missing wrathful attributes. The only missing line of the acrostic of Psalm 145 is the נ line.[94] Pigott suggests that any of the three *qal* participles associated with Exod 34:7 (נֹצֵר; נֹשֵׂא; נַקֵּה) could have originally begun the *nun* line.[95] Pigott's pro-

---

91. Holm-Nielson, "*Importance* of *Late Jewish Psalmody*," 40–41.

92. Pigott, "God of Compassion and Mercy," 186.

93. Ibid., 186.

94. In a version of Psalm 145 in 11QPsa the missing line is replaced by a later edition that uses "Elohim" instead of the normal "YHWH" of the Psalm. The LXX follows 11QPsa with the translation of "Elohim" with "kurios."

95. Pigott, "God of Compassion and Mercy," 186. Pigott affirms the fact that there is no manuscript evidence to support the hypothesis, but simply offers it as an interesting proposal.

posal is both interesting and creative, but ultimately unfounded. There is no manuscript evidence to support this proposal. Furthermore, it seems unlikely that the psalmist would have separated the two poles of the credo by five lines. The psalmist only once mentions a characteristic which might be deemed wrathful (145:20)—"YHWH guards over all of those who love him, but all of the evil ones are destroyed." In this case, the merciful and wrathful attributes are juxtaposed. If the poet had wished to announce YHWH's wrathful side by using the credo, then the attributes would have been connected to the merciful attributes given.

Ultimately, the form taken for this parallel of the credo can be explained using many of the same reasons as given for the parallel in Psalm 103. The psalmist wished only to recall the positive, merciful attributes of YHWH for the minds of the readers. The psalmist continually makes reference to YHWH's mighty acts—the attributes are given as some of these acts. By only referring to the merciful attributes of YHWH, the psalmist indirectly asserts that only the positive aspects of YHWH's reign will be rehearsed by the "generations" (145:4). This implicit assertion sees only the merciful attributes being told when the future generations "tell of the glory of your kingdom" (145:11).

Participation in the Larger Context

Psalm 145 proclaims the divine sovereignty of YHWH over the psalmist (145:1), all creatures (145:10) and all flesh (145:21). While some psalms affirm that YHWH is both "my God and my King" (Ps 5:3; 84:4), only Psalm 145 uses the definite article to proclaim, "My God the King."[96] In addition to the alphabetic acrostic that governs the poem, Wilfred Watson finds a secondary mini-acrostic in 145:11–13 that asserts YHWH's kingship.[97] Watson suggests that the effect of inversing the root מלך is "to reverse the flow of time and so depict eternity."[98] I believe that Watson's argument is appealing and not simply a quirk of the normal alphabetic ordering in acrostics.[99] In 145:11–13, the root occurs four times out of only five appearances in the entire psalm (cf. 145:1). This

96. Kimelman, "Psalm 145," 38.

97. Watson, "Reversed Rootplay in Ps 145," 101–2.

98. Ibid., 102.

99. Any acrostic would have a "reverse rootplay" in the ך, ל, and מ lines that spell out "king."

increased density of the root in these verses shows the mini-acrostic to be a "theme" of the psalm and not simply a quirk.

In addition to the frame of the poem built upon the acrostic, an inclusio also exists which gives the necessary response to YHWH's reign—to "praise." The psalm begins with the heading "A Praise (תְהִלָּה) of David" and is the only psalm in the Psalter to bear the title of "A Praise."[100] The psalm ends with the affirmation that "a praise of YHWH" will be on the psalmist's lips (145:21) forming the inclusio. The inclusio marks the appropriate response to YHWH's kingship. Dahood also finds an inclusio with the exclamation, "I will praise your name forever and ever" (145:2) and the final assertion of the psalm that "all flesh will bless his holy name forever and ever" (145:21).[101] These major and minor inclusios in the psalm show that the natural reaction when confronted with YHWH's sovereignty is praise.

A third structural component of Psalm 145 is the repetition of key words. Leon Liebreich argues that בָּרַךְ is the defining key word of the psalm.[102] Liebreich finds a progression from the praises of the psalmist (145:1–2), to the praises of all the saints (145:10), before the psalm ends with "all flesh" praising YHWH (145:21).[103] This repetition divides the poem into two major sections (145:3–9; 11–20) by a Prelude (145:1–2), an Interlude (145:10) and a Postlude (145:21) all three of which are governed by the root בָּרַךְ.[104]

The parallel of the credo comes in 145:8 in the first major section. After the prelude where the psalmist declares her intentions to praise YHWH, the first section declares that all generations will speak God's praises. The first four verses (145:3–7) make this claim in various ways after the generic statement that "YHWH is great" (145:3). The "generations" to come will "praise," "tell," "celebrate" and "sing" of God's "works," "greatness" and "mighty acts" (145:4–7). The psalmist simply asserts that these different groups, and the psalmist himself, will commemorate YHWH's goodness. Kimelman sees within this "thesaurus of adulation" a "structure of intensification, not simply a juggling of semantic

---

100. Dahood, *Psalms III*, 336.

101. Ibid., 339. See also Weiser, *The Psalms*, 207–8, who finds a connection between the phrases that begin and end the psalm.

102. Liebreich, "Psalms 34 and 145," 187–90.

103. Ibid., 187–88.

104. Ibid., 187–88. See also Kimelman, "Psalm 145," 38.

equivalents."[105] He draws from this intensification an assertion by the psalmist that "the loftiest encomium proves to be an understatement."[106]

The credo comes in 145:8 as the actual substance of this proclamation of praise from the people. The credo which centers on YHWH's compassion and mercy, greatness in loving kindness and aversion to anger is the liturgy used to recall God's mighty acts. This liturgy of compassion stands in contrast to recitations of YHWH's historical acts such as von Rad's *kleine credo*. McCann sees within the message an astounding assertion that God's power is manifest in motherly love.[107] His thesis is supported by the fact that the compassion (רחם) of YHWH is the only attribute mentioned twice (145:8–9) and forms the basis of what the praise will entail. Ultimately, the credo asserts that YHWH is good, not because of the Exodus or creation, but because of God's compassionate and gracious character.

The second key word of Psalm 145 is "all" (כל) which occurs sixteen times. The continuous repetition of the term emphasizes the totality of those who will praise God and the reasons for which YHWH should be praised.[108] As mentioned above, the "bless" structure of the psalm opens ever wider from the psalmist, to all the saints, before a final exclamation that all flesh should praise YHWH. As with the other parallels of the credo in the Psalter, this parallel connects the attributes of YHWH with God's interactions with all of creation. As opposed to the intimate connection of YHWH and ancient Israel in the Torah and to the intermediary position of the Twelve which contains exclusivist and inclusivist positions, this parallel accepts the position that YHWH is king over the entire cosmos without reservation.

Psalm 145 also stands as an important psalm in the overall shape of the Psalter. The psalm concludes Book V and is the last psalm of the Psalter before the final five "hallel" psalms which end it. The acrostic structure of the psalm alerts the reader that all has been said about YHWH's reign; every argument from א to ת has been made to show that YHWH is king.[109] The complete nature of an acrostic lets the reader

---

105. Kimelman, "Psalm 145," 43.

106. Ibid., 43.

107. McCann, "Psalms," 1260.

108. Mays, *Psalms*, 438.

109. DeClaissé-Walford, *Reading from the Beginning*, 99.

know that the psalmist has given a comprehensive, motivational list to elicit praise. The ending of Psalm 145 urges all flesh to praise YHWH. The five *hallel* psalms that end the Psalter answer this call and build toward the crescendo of Psalm 150.[110]

Gerald Wilson has outlined three ways that Psalm 145 stands as the climax of Book V.[111] First, it connects the ways of the righteous and wicked of Psalms 1 and 107 with the admonitions of 145:20. The dualistic nature of "those who love" vis-à-vis "the wicked" matches both the beginning of the Psalter and the beginning of Book V. Second, thematic connections exist between major psalms in Book IV. The themes of the kingship of YHWH (145:1, 11–13↔93:1–2; 99:1–5), the "mighty acts" of YHWH (145:4–7↔92:5–9; 96:3–4) and the "loving kindness" of YHWH (145:8–9, 13–20↔103:6–13; 107:4–9) all show Psalm 145 to be an answer to the questions raised by Book IV. Third, Psalm 145 answers the refrain of Psalm 107 that celebrates YHWH's loving kindness.

I would add two further ways that Psalm 145 stands as a climax of Book V. Psalm 145 is "of David" as are both Psalms 86 and 103. The superscription places this final call to praise YHWH as the eternal King within the mouth of ancient Israel's iconic earthly king David. Nancy deClaissé-Walford expands on the irony, "If David, to whom any hope of fulfillment of the promises he was given by God seems forever lost, if David can remember and praise God and pass that memory along, then all Israel can and must do the same."[112] If one accepts the fact that the Psalter is a large lament over the Davidic monarchy, then the final call to praise from David would have resonated with the readers. Second, the psalm is entitled a "praise" (תהלה) and is the only psalm to be so titled in the Psalter. This uniqueness marks the psalm as an important closure to the Psalter and that its core message (YHWH is king) demands praise.

Based upon the above analysis, there are four summary statements to be made:

1. The psalm is from the postexilic period and would have encouraged the people ravaged by competing kingdoms to put their trust in YHWH.

---

110. Wilson, *The Editing of the Hebrew Psalter*, 194.

111. Ibid., 225–27.

112. DeClaissé-Walford, *Reading from the Beginning*, 98–99.

2. The credo only rehearses the compassionate attributes of YHWH with an almost exact quotation of Ps 103:8.

3. The credo forms the basis of what the praise of the psalmist would be in the first major section of Psalm 145. The psalmist turns to the credo as the core affirmations of YHWH's reign over all of creation.

4. Psalm 145 stands in a climactic place within the structure of the Psalter as a final, triumphant exclamation that YHWH's kingdom has neither temporal nor spatial boundaries.

CONCLUSIONS

The final section of this chapter will outline some summary statements about the function of the parallels of the credo within the Psalter. The section will first outline diachronic conclusions, then move to examine the synchronic contributions of the parallels to the Psalter.

Diachronic Results

It was shown that each parallel of the credo in the Psalter is in a psalm that is postexilic. Psalm 86 was shown to be a late composition that relied heavily upon earlier works for its final form. Psalm 103 was also thought to be late because of borrowing from exilic/postexilic sources. Psalm 145 was found to be late because of Aramaic endings and connections with other psalms. The collection of parallels in the Psalter stands as some of the latest parallels in the Hebrew Bible.

Wilson has argued that the Psalter did not reach its final form until late in the first century CE.[113] As noted above, Wilson's main argument arises from the collections of psalms found at Qumran.[114] In these collections, the first three books (Psalms 1–89) were set by the time of Qumran while the last two books exhibit some fluidity. Wilson uses this data to show that the first three books of the Psalter had reached a point of stabilization before Qumran, but that the final form of the whole was not achieved until the first century CE.

113. Wilson, "A First Century CE Date," 102–10. See also Holladay, *The Psalms through Three Thousand Years*, 136–43.

114. For an overview of the psalms present at Qumran see Sanders, *The Dead Sea Psalms Scroll*, 13–14; and Wilson, *Editing of the Hebrew Psalter*, 121.

On the other hand, Hossfeld and Zenger argue that the final redaction of the Psalter had occurred by 200 BCE.[115] Hossfeld and Zenger note the fact that both the LXX and the Hebrew Psalter contain 150 psalms and that Psalms 1, 2, and 149 are associated from an early time as introductions and conclusion to the Psalter. As a middle position, I believe that deClaissé-Walford offers the most tenable hypothesis.[116] She holds that, "The Psalter achieved its 'substantial' form sometime in the late Persian/early Greek period (late 4th century)."[117] She suggests that the "story line" was in place by this time, but that the actual shape of Books IV and V was not set by the first century CE. The evidence from Qumran shows that the psalms of Books IV to V were contained in the collections but not in their current order. While deClaissé-Walford's assertion that the "story line" was in place by late fourth century is correct, I believe that the story would have been strengthened by the final order of the books which was not achieved until the first century CE.

A second diachronic result from this analysis is that it has shown that the parallels of the credo are more truncated than either those of the Torah or the Twelve. For the first time, these parallels offer no mention of the wrathful attributes of YHWH. The closeness of each parallel may be a sign that this compassionate version of the credo may have been part of the standard position of those who urged the nation not to assimilate, but to stay faithful to YHWH in spite of the political difficulties of the nation. From the late Persian period to the Roman destruction of Jerusalem in 70 CE, the nation never experienced complete political stability. The Persians, Greeks and Romans all imposed their ideologies onto the ancient Israelites and the three psalms containing parallels to the credo could have functioned to counter the propaganda of the foreign monarchs. The fact that each of the three parallels contains a similar use of the original may show that the propaganda of the faithful emphasized the merciful and compassionate nature of YHWH. This message would have been effective during any time from the fourth century BCE to the first century CE.

The result of the combination of these two hypotheses is that the each of the psalms which contain the credo likely reached its final form

115. Hossfeld and Zenger, *Die Psalmen I, Psalm 1–50*, 8–9.

116. DeClaissé-Walford, *Reading from the Beginning*, 19.

117. Ibid., 19n11.

before the Psalter reached its final form. A similar quotation to the three major parallels of the Psalter is located in Neh 9:17.[118] While critical discussion of Nehemiah has found no consensus by the scholarly community, it is agreed by most that the book originated roughly between 400 and 300 BCE.[119] This similarity between the parallel in Nehemiah and those in the Psalter may help to give a date for the parallels in the psalms. Furthermore, it may indicate that this version of the credo was rhetoric used in anti-assimilation circles during the late Persian and early Greek periods.[120]

Synchronic Results

Synchronically, our analysis has shown that each parallel played a major role in its psalm. The parallel in Psalm 86 comes as part of a stair step doxological structure with the parallel forming the climactic doxology of the poem. In Psalm 103, the parallel of the credo and echoes of the credo provide structure to the five strophes of the psalm. In Psalm 145, the parallel forms the substance of the praise promised and demanded by the psalm. In each instance, the parallel helps to shape the psalm.

The above analysis has also shown that the location of each parallel and the attributes rehearsed are used to enunciate the compassionate rule of YHWH over the entire cosmos. All three appearances in the Psalter come in psalms that proclaim the rule of YHWH over all of creation. The

118. It adds "you are God" and "you have not forsaken them" to the attributes. Otherwise, it is a very close parallel.

119. The central issue in dating Nehemiah revolves around the chronological relationship between the historical figures of Ezra and Nehemiah. If one takes the canonical chronology of Ezra preceding Nehemiah, then one can date the text around 400 BCE. For example, Derek Kidner, *Ezra and Nehemiah*, 14, accepts the canonical order (Ezra arrived in Jerusalem about 458 BCE with Nehemiah following roughly three years later) and believes that Nehemiah was penned sometime toward the end Darius' reign in 404 BCE. On the other hand, some hold that the Artaxerxes mentioned in Ezra 4:7 may refer to Artaxerxes II (404–358 BCE), which would mean that Ezra was after Nehemiah. This rearrangement would place the date of Nehemiah sometime in the late fourth century. The origins of this view can be traced to Bright, *A History of Israel*, 400–401. For a full review of these issues, see Williamson, *Ezra, Nehemiah*, xxxix–xliv; Blenkinsopp, *Ezra, Nehemiah*, 47–54; and Duggan, *The Covenant Renewal in Ezra-Nehemiah*, 1–30.

120. Literarily the credo comes in Ezra's prayer that YHWH might forgive their sinful assimilation in the same way that the ancient Israelites were forgiven during the time of the past.

similarity of the parallels shows that the theology of the Psalter assumes a certain set of fixed attributes to be associated with YHWH's reign, namely "compassionate and gracious," "slow to anger," and "great in loving kindness." The only deviation from these attributes is that Psalm 86 adds that YHWH is great in "truth." In this way, the Psalter contains the most consistent rehearsals of any section of the Hebrew Bible. There is also a thematic consistency as each parallel proclaims the reign of YHWH.

The analyses have shown that the locations of the three parallels participate in the overall shape of the Psalter by emphasizing the reign of YHWH over the cosmos. In Book III, Psalm 86 (along with Psalm 87) tempers the harshness of the overall shape of the Book and the final four psalms in particular which lament the demise of the Davidic monarchy that comes in Psalms 88–89. In Book IV, Psalm 103 again foreshadows the universal reign of YHWH that dominates Book V. Psalm 103, paired with Psalm 104, uses creation imagery to praise YHWH. Furthermore, the psalm also exhibits thematic connections with the final two psalms of Book IV (Psalms 105–106) with the mention of Moses and the mighty deeds of YHWH toward ancient Israel. In Book V, Psalm 145 concludes the Book with a climactic call to praise and thematic connections with the rest of the Psalter.

A final synchronic feature comes as each psalm that contains a parallel of the credo begins with a superscription "of David." Psalm 86 contains the only Davidic superscription in Book III. Psalm 103 is one of only two psalms in Book IV to have the Davidic superscription. While there are many psalms in Book V to use the Davidic superscription, only Psalm 145 uses "a praise of David." This close connection between the appearances of the credo and David shows that in the final theology of the Psalter ancient Israel's most celebrated earthly king supports the reign of YHWH.

5

Conclusions and Prospects for Further Study

INTRODUCTION

This chapter will look for conclusions and general themes that have arisen from the explorations of the locations of the parallels of the credo in the Torah, the Twelve and the Psalter. Special attention will be paid to the theological emphasis of the credo and the significance of the credo for each passage in which it is located. I will also look for general diachronic trajectories that may be present in the canon. The chapter will end with prospects for further study.

Synchronic Conclusions

The major thesis of this work is that the canonical locations of the parallels move from an emphasis on YHWH and ancient Israel's covenant relationship toward highlighting YHWH's reign over the entire cosmos. In the Torah, the use of the credo highlights contexts that portray YHWH and ancient Israel as intimate covenant partners. The parallels from the two versions of the Decalogue in Exodus 20 and Deuteronomy 5 both affirm ancient Israel's role in keeping the covenant. Exodus 34 and Numbers 14, however, show that ancient Israel's obedience is only penultimate; the relationship ultimately relies on YHWH's compassion and mercy. All four appearances of the credo in the Torah focus strictly on the interaction of ancient Israel and YHWH. The relationship is further accentuated by YHWH's portrayal as "jealous" of ancient Israel's devotion in the Torah. The nations are never thought of being in the same type of relationship as YHWH and ancient Israel.[1] This emphasis is further highlighted by the fact that the parallels occur at significant junctures in the covenantal narrative.

A significant change occurs as the reader comes to the next canonical parallels of the credo found in the Twelve. In the Twelve, the relationship between YHWH and ancient Israel shows open interaction with the other nations and evidences a significant shift from the emphasis of the Torah. In Joel 2, the prophet uses the attributes of YHWH to show that God will come to the aid of ancient Israel, effectively silencing the taunts of the other nations. The book of Micah ends with a hymn based upon the credo which asserts that YHWH's compassion will eventually prove to be ancient Israel's salvation. A different perspective is offered in Jonah 4 which uses the credo to show that God's compassion is available to the other nations. The inclusivist position is rebuffed by a use of the credo in Nahum 1 which proclaims that YHWH's wrath will be visited upon Nineveh.

Another significant step is taken in the progression as the reader comes to the parallels of the credo in the Psalter which all proclaim the reign of YHWH over the entire cosmos. Psalms 86, 103, and 145 all use parallels of the credo to affirm that YHWH's reign is marked by a merciful nature which is "compassionate and gracious," "slow to anger," and "great in loving kindness." All three psalms are located on or in close connection with the "seams" between the books. These three psalms assume God's rule over all. Only once in the three psalms is ancient Israel mentioned (103:7) and then only as a past example of YHWH's mighty acts.

Parallels of the credo do not appear in every book of the canon. It is significant, however, that they do appear in every section of the canon. The parallels dominate the covenantal narrative of the Torah and appear in three of the five books. In the Prophets, parallels are only present in the Twelve, but these parallels span several centuries and give continuity to the first half of the Twelve. They also provide an important link between the first and second halves of the Twelve. In the Writings, the majority of the parallels appear in the Psalter. The Psalter is the preeminent book of the Writings and sometimes even functions as a synecdoche marking

---

1. The closest appearance of the nations in the immediate context of the four parallels in the Torah comes in Num 14:15.

this third part of the canon.[2] I believe the significance of the locations of the parallels shows a canonical movement which emphasizes YHWH's reign over the entire cosmos.

A second synchronic observation came as the analyses of the parallels showed that each of the eleven parallels is "significant" for its immediate context. There were three different varieties of significance found in the parallels' relationships to their contexts. First, the study found several of the parallels to come in turning points in their narrative/context. In Exodus 34, the credo comes at the climactic point in the narrative in the theophany of YHWH. In Numbers 14, Moses reminds YHWH of the attributes of the credo as the reason why the ancient Israelites should be forgiven. In Joel 2, the parallel of the credo comes at the theological fulcrum of the book which sees a shift from judgment to hope. The parallel of the credo in Jonah 4 explains to the reader the reason for the prophet's peculiar behavior.

Second, we noted the significance of parallels found at beginnings and endings. In Exodus 20 and Deuteronomy 5, the credo is connected to the first two commandments of the Decalogue. Both parallels begin long sections of legal material. The parallel of Nahum 1 comes at the very beginning of the book and the א portion of the acrostic. In Micah 7, the hymn based upon the credo ends the book.

Third, several parallels were found in contexts where the attributes of the credo saturated the entire pericope. In Psalm 86, the attributes form part of the stair step parallelism that governs the book. In Psalm 103, in addition to the major parallel in 103:8, echoes of the credo appear in four of the five sections of the psalm. Psalm 145, which stands as a final affirmation in Book V that all flesh shall praise YHWH, uses the credo as the substance of the praise of all flesh. In each of these three varieties of "significance," the parallels of the credo all form part of the essential fabric of their immediate context. In no place does the credo seem to be an awkward secondary addition or clumsy late insertion.

A third synchronic observation was found in that each parallel shaped the attributes of the original for its context. While there were certainly some deviations from understanding the form of the parallels to be governed strictly by context, overall the shape of each parallel arose from

2. For example, see Luke 24:44, which refers to "The Law, the Prophets and the Psalms," and 4Q MMT which uses the title of "The Law, the Prophets and David."

the theological needs of the book. Susan Pigott's work demonstrated the theological balance of each parallel, but this volume has focused more on the contextualization of each parallel.[3] While Pigott's work sought balance in each rehearsal of the original in order to combat contemporary Marcionite tendencies of the church, I have focused on how the individual writers crafted the credo to support their various theological agendas.

For example, the parallels of Exodus 20 and Deuteronomy 5 invert the order of the poles of the credo to emphasize the potential for wrath if the covenant is violated. Other texts such as Exodus 34, Numbers 14 and Micah 7 all suggest that the survival of the nation rests in the loving kindness of YHWH. Nahum marshals God's wrathful characteristics as a warning to the Ninevites; while at the opposite end of the spectrum, Psalm 145 announces the compassionate rule of YHWH over the cosmos. The theological diversity of the different manifestations of the credo is remarkable.

Diachronic Conclusions

The diachronic portion of this study focused on finding the earliest time when it could reasonably be said that a parallel could be associated with its context. From this study three central affirmations can be made. First, the different pericopes ranged in time from sometime late in the monarchy (Exodus 34) to postexilic (Psalm 86; 145). This diversity of dating shows that the tradition represented by the credo maintained continuous strength and influence among the ancient Israelites. The attributes of the credo were a central part of the core theological affirmations of the nation during some of the most formative times of the people.

Second, a trajectory which witnesses the abbreviation of the later parallels was found. The earliest appearances of the credo exhibit the fullest quotation of the attributes. In fact, four of the earliest parallels are the only four to manifest the balance of Exod 34:6–7. All of the later parallels concentrate on either the compassionate or wrathful pole of the credo. In addition to this shift from theological balance to monolithic affirmation, the earliest quotations are also the longest. A diachronic movement can be seen where the later communities redacted the attributes to focus exclusively on the compassionate nature of YHWH by completely omitting the wrathful pole. This movement from longer to shorter stands in

3. Pigott, "God of Compassion and Mercy."

direct opposition to von Rad's ideas about the *kleine credo* which grew from shorter to longer.[4]

Third, the diversity of the theological shaping of the different parallels shows that ancient Israel was not a uniform, homogenous whole, but rather composed of varied, diverse groups. The differences give evidence of the theological diversity present in ancient Israel. While finding theological diversity in a group the size of ancient Israel is not surprising, it is remarkable that at no point did the competing groups excise their theological opponents' positions in the sacred texts. For example, in the Twelve the diverse opinions of both Jonah and Joel are included in the final canonical form. The intense exclusivity of the parallels of the Torah opposes the universal vision of YHWH's reign that the credo highlights in the Psalter. The final form of the text stands as evidence that at no point was the theological tension between YHWH's mercy and grace fully resolved by the larger community of ancient Israel; the diversity of parallels record the various groups' theological struggles.

PROSPECTS FOR FUTURE STUDY

I believe that this study opens avenues for research in three areas. First, I have attempted a "canonical approach" that combines both diachronic and synchronic methodologies. There could be other topics to be explored which stand as major canonical themes, but also exhibit some diachronic development such as studies on the patriarchs/matriarchs or the monarchy. Second, the function of minor echoes of the credo in the shape and shaping of the canon need exploration, especially the word pairs "loving kindness and truth" (חסד ואמת) and "compassionate and gracious" (רחם וחנון). Third, the comparison of the parallels could provide clarity in dating passages which contain the credo. A secondary part of this analysis could explore the rhetoric of the anti-assimilation party of the late Persian/early Greek periods which used the credo in the three parallels in the Psalter and the parallel in Nehemiah.

FINAL THOUGHTS

The theological significance of this study for the contemporary church stands in the application of both diachronic and synchronic truths. This

---

4. Von Rad, "The Form-Critical Problem of the Hexateuch," 1–78.

canonical analysis has shown that the ancient Israelites took the old traditions of the credo as normative, but at the same time shaped and crafted that tradition to meet their theological needs. Contemporary theologian Paul Fiddes has argued that the Christian canon provides a fence which provides theological boundaries for the church, but also allows differentiation within the boundaries.[5] Another contemporary theologian, Robert Jensen makes a similar argument regarding Christian creeds, "An irreversible rule of faith is dogma. It sets the bounds of what can pass as the proper message of the community. For theology, the bounds of the permissible will be set by the metarule [the creeds]: no proposed theologoumenon [theological opinion] can be true that would hinder a dogma's control of the church's discourse."[6]

It is my belief that the canonical analysis of the credo provides a model for today's fractured church. The ancient Israelites took seriously and actively engaged the traditional texts, but at the same time allowed dialogue surrounding these texts. The result of this hermeneutic was a vibrant and diverse community which was held together by its common textual traditions, but which also allowed serious contention for divergent theological positions. The canonization of all positions side by side is a call to the contemporary church to embrace the tension which results from accepting old traditions while still bravely exploring contemporary horizons.

5. Fiddes, "The Canon as Space and Place," 127–49.

6. Jensen, *The Triune God*, 36.

Bibliography

Ackerman, James. "Satire and Symbolism in the Book of Jonah." In *Traditions in Transformation: Turning Points in Biblical Faith*, edited by Baruch Halpern and Jon D. Levenson, 213–46. Winona Lake, IN: Eisenbrauns, 1981.

Ahlström, G. W. *Joel and the Temple Cult of Jerusalem*. Supplements to Vetus Testamentum 21. Leiden: Brill, 1971.

Alexander, T. Desmond. "Jonah." In *Obadiah, Jonah, Micah: An Introduction and Commentary*, by David W. Baker, T. Desmond Alexander, and Bruce Waltke, 47–134. Tyndale Old Testament Commentary. Downers Grove, IL: InterVarsity, 1988.

Allen, Leslie C. *The Books of Joel, Obadiah, Jonah and Micah*. New International Commentary on the Old Testament. Grand Rapids: Eerdmans, 1976.

———. *Psalms 101–150*. Word Biblical Commentary 21. Waco, TX: 1983.

Allis, Oswald T. "Nahum, Nineveh, Elkosh." *Evangelical Quarterly* 27 (1955) 67–80.

Alt, Albrecht. "The Origins of Israelite Law." In *Essays on Old Testament History and Religion*, translated by R. A. Wilson, 101–71. Garden City, NY: Doubleday, 1967.

Anderson, Francis I., and David N. Freedman. *Micah: A New Translation with Introduction and Commentary*. Anchor Bible 24E. New York: Doubleday, 2000.

———. "'Prose Particle' Counts of the Hebrew Bible." In *The Word of the Lord Shall Go Forth*, edited by Carol L. Meyers and M. O'Connor, 165–83. Winona Lake, IN: Eisenbrauns, 1983.

Anderson, A. A. *The Book of Psalms*. Vol. 2, *Psalms 73–150*. New Century Bible. London: Oliphants, 1972.

Ap-Thomas, D. R. "Some Aspects of the Root HNN in the Old Testament." *Journal of Semitic Studies* 2 (1957) 140–41.

Ashley, Timothy R. *The Book of Numbers*. New International Commentary on the Old Testament. Grand Rapids: Eerdmans, 1993.

Bailey, Waylon. "Nahum." In *Micah, Nahum, Habakkuk, Zephaniah*, by Kenneth L. Barker and Walon Bailey, 137–243. New American Commentary 20. Nashville: Broadman & Holman, 1998.

Bakhtin, Mikhail. "Carnival Ambivalence." In *The Bakhtin Reader: Selected Writings of Bakhtin, Medvedev, Voloshinov*, edited by Pam Morris, 206–26. New York: Oxford University Press, 1994.

———. *The Dialogic Imagination: Four Essays*. Edited by Michael Holquist. Translated by Cheryl Emerson and Michael Holquist. University of Texas Press Slavic Series 1. Austin: University of Texas Press, 2002.

Balentine, Samuel E. *The Torah's Vision of Worship*. Overtures to Biblical Theology. Minneapolis: Fortress, 1999.

Baltzer, Klaus. *The Covenant Formulary: In Old Testament, Jewish and Early Christian Writings*. Translated by David Green. Philadelphia: Fortress, 1971.

Barton, John. *Joel and Obadiah: A Commentary*. Old Testament Library. Louisville: Westminster John Knox, 2001.

Beckwith, Roger T. *The Old Testament Canon of the New Testament Church and Its Background in Early Judaism*. Grand Rapids: Eerdmans, 1985.

Bellinger, W. H., Jr. *Leviticus and Numbers*. New International Biblical Commentary on the Old Testament 3. Peabody, MA: Hendrickson, 2001.

———. *Psalms: Reading and Studying the Book of Praises*. Peabody, MA: Hendrickson, 1990.

Ben Zvi, Ehu. *Micah*. Forms of Old Testament Literature 21B. Grand Rapids: Eerdmans, 2000.

———. "Twelve Prophetic Books or 'The Twelve': A Few Preliminary Considerations." In *Forming Prophetic Literature: Essays on Isaiah and the Twelve in Honor of John D. W. Watts*, edited by James W. Watts and Paul R. House, 125–56. Journal for the Study of the Old Testament Supplement Series 235. Sheffield, UK: Sheffield Academic, 1996.

Berquist, Jon L. *Judaism in Persia's Shadow: A Social and Historical Approach*. Reprinted, Eugene, OR: Wipf & Stock, 2003. 1995.

Bewer, Julius A. "A Critical and Exegetical Commentary on Jonah." In *A Critical an Exegetical Commentary on Haggai, Zechariah, Malachi and Jonah*, 3–65. Interpreters Critical Commentary 25. Edinburgh: T. & T. Clark, 1912.

Beyerlin, Walter. *Die Kulttraditionen Israels in der Verkündigung des Propheten Micha*. Göttingern: Vandenhoeck & Ruprecht, 1959.

———. *Origins and History of the Oldest Sinaitic Traditions*. Translated by S. Rudman. Oxford: Blackwell, 1965.

Biddle, Mark E. "'Israel' and 'Jacob' in the Book of Micah: Micah in the Context of the Twelve." in *Reading and Hearing the Book of the Twelve*, edited by James D. Nogalski and Marvin A. Sweeney, 146–65. SBL Symposium Series 15. Atlanta: Society of Biblical Literature, 2000.

Blenkinsopp, Joseph. *Ezra-Nehemiah: A Commentary*. The Old Testament Library. Philadelphia: Westminster, 1988.

———. *The Pentateuch: An Introduction to the First Five Books of the Bible*. The Anchor Bible Reference Library. New York: Doubleday, 1992.

Boorer, Suzanne. *The Promise of the Land as Oath: A Key to the Formation of the Pentateuch*. Beihefte zur Zeitschrift für die alttestamentliche Wissenschaft 205. Berlin: de Gruyter, 1992.

Botterweck, G. Johannes and Helmer Ringgren, editors. *Theological Dictionary of the Old Testament*. Translated by John T. Willis et al. 15 vols. Grand Rapids: Eerdmans, 1974.

Braulik, G. "The Sequence of the Laws in Deuteronomy 12–26 and in the Decalogue." In *A Song of Power and the Power of Song: Essays on the Book of Deuteronomy*, edited by Duane Christenson, 313–35. Sources for Biblical and Theological Study 3. Winona Lake, IN: Eisenbrauns, 1993.

Briggs, Charles A. *A Critical and Exegetical Commentary on the Book of Psalms*, vol. 2. International Critical Commentary 15. New York: Scribner, 1909.

Bright, John. *A History of Israel*. 3rd ed. Philadelphia: Westminster, 1981.

Brueggemann, Walter. "Bounded by Obedience and Praise: The Psalms as Canon." In *The Psalms and the Life of Faith*, by Walter Brueggemann, edited by Patrick D. Miller, 189–213. Minneapolis: Fortress, 1995.

———. "Crisis-Evoked, Crisis-Resolving Speech." *Biblical Theology Bulletin* 24 (1994) 95–105.

———. *Deuteronomy.* Abingdon Old Testament Commentaries. Nashville: Abingdon, 2001.

———. *The Message of the Psalms: A Theological Commentary.* Augsburg Old Testament Studies. Minneapolis: Augsburg, 1984.

———. *Theology of the Old Testament: Testimony, Dispute, Advocacy.* Minneapolis: Fortress, 1997.

Brueggemann, Walter, and Patrick D. Miller. "Psalm 73 as a Canonical Marker." *Journal for the Study of the Old Testament* 72 (1996) 45–56.

Burnett, Joel S. "The Question of Divine Absence in Israelite and West Semitic Religion." *Catholic Biblical Quarterly* 67 (2005) 215–35.

Buttenwieser, Moses. *The Psalms: Chronologically Treated with a New Translation.* The Library of Biblical Studies. New York: Ktav, 1969.

Carmichael, Calum M. *Laws of Deuteronomy.* Ithaca: Cornell University Press, 1974.

Carson, D. A., and H. G. M. Williamson, editors. *It Is Written: Scripture Citing Scripture. Essays in Honor of Barnabas Lindars, SSF.* Cambridge: Cambridge University Press, 1988.

Cassuto, U. *A Commentary on the Book of Exodus.* Translated by Israel Abrahams. Publications of the Perry Foundation for Biblical Research in the Hebrew University of Jerusalem. Jerusalem: Magnes, 1967.

———."The Sequence and Arrangement of the Biblical Sections." In *Biblical and Oriental Studies,* translated by Israel Abrams. Vol. 1, *The Bible,* 1–6. Publications of the Perry Foundation for Biblical Research in the Hebrew University of Jerusalem. Jerusalem: Magnes, 1973.

Childs, Brevard S. *Introduction to the Old Testament as Scripture.* Philadelphia: Fortress, 1979.

———. *The Book of Exodus: A Critical, Theological Commentary.* Old Testament Library. Philadelphia: Westminster, 1974.

Clark, Gordon R. *The Word* Hesed *in the Hebrew Bible.* Journal for the Study of the Old Testament Supplement Series 157. Sheffield, UK: JSOT Press, 1993.

Clements, Ronald E. "Patterns in the Prophetic Canon." In *Canon and Authority: Essays in Old Testament Religion and Theology,* edited by George W. Coats and Burke O. Long, 42–55. Philadelphia: Fortress, 1977.

Clines, David J. A. *The Theme of the Pentateuch.* 2nd ed. Journal for the Study of the Old Testament Supplement Series 10 Sheffield, UK: JSOT Press, 1997.

Coats, George W. *Rebellion in the Wilderness: The Murmuring Motif in the Wilderness, Traditions of the Old Testament.* Nashville: Abingdon, 1968.

Coggins, R. J. "An Alternative Prophetic Tradition?" In *Israel's Prophetic Tradition: Essays in Honour of Peter R. Ackroyd,* edited by Richard Coggins, et al., 77–94. Cambridge: Cambridge University Press, 1982.

Credner, Karl A. *Der Prophet Joel übersetzt und erklärt.* Halle: n.p., 1831.

Crenshaw, James L. *Joel: A New Translation with Introduction and Commentary.* Anchor Bible. 24C. New York: Doubleday, 1995.

———. "Theodicy in the Book of the Twelve." In *Thematic Threads in the Book of the Twelve,* edited by Paul L. Redditt and Aaron Schart, 175–91. Beihefte zur Zeitschrift für die alttestamentliche Wissenschaft 325. New York: de Gruyter, 2003.

Curtis, Byron G. "The Zion-Daughter Oracles: Evidence on the Identity and Ideology of the Late Redactors of the Book of the Twelve." In *Reading and Hearing the Book of the Twelve,* edited by James D. Nogalski and Marvin A. Sweeney, 166–84. SBL Symposium Series 15. Atlanta: Society of Biblical Literature, 2000.

Dahood, Mitchell. *Psalms: Introduction, Translation and Notes.* Vol. 2, *Psalms 51–100.* Anchor Bible 17. Garden City, NY: Doubleday, 1968.

———. *Psalms: Introduction, Translation and Notes.* Vol. 3, *Psalms 101–150.* Anchor Bible 17A. Garden City, NY: Doubleday, 1970.

DeClaissé-Walford, Nancy. *Introduction to the Psalms: A Song from Ancient Israel.* St. Louis: Chalice, 2004.

———. *Reading from the Beginning: The Shaping of the Hebrew Psalter.* Macon, GA: Mercer University Press, 1997.

Delitzsch, Franz J. "Wann weissagte Obadja?" *Zeitschrift fürdie lutherische Theologie und Kirche* 12 (1851) 91–102.

Dentan, Robert C. "The Literary Affinities of Exodus XXXIV 6f." *Vetus Testamentum* 13 (1963) 34–51.

Dillard, Raymond B. "Joel." In *The Minor Prophets: An Exegetical and Expository Commentary* Vol. 1, *Hosea, Joel, and Amos,* edited by Thomas E. McComiskey, 239–313. Grand Rapids: Baker, 1992.

Dozeman, Thomas B. "Inner-Biblical Interpretation of Yahweh's Gracious and Compassionate Character." *Journal of Biblical Literature* 108 (1989) 207–23.

Driver, S. R. *Introduction to the Literature of the Old Testament.* 9th ed. International Theological Library 1. Edinburgh: T. & T. Clark, 1913.

Duggan, Michael W. *The Covenant Renewal in Ezra-Nehemiah (Neh 7:72b—10:40) An Exegetical, Literary and Theological Study.* SBL Dissertation Series 164. Atlanta: Society of Biblical Literature, 2001.

Duhm, Bernhard. "Anmerkungen zu den Zwölf Propheten." *Zeitschrift für die alttestamentliche Wissenschaft* 31 (1911) 161–204.

Eaton, J. H. *Psalms.* Torch Bible Commentaries. London: SCM, 1967.

Eissfeldt, Otto. *The Old Testament: An Introduction.* Translated by Peter R. Ackroyd. New York: Harper & Row, 1965.

Ellison, H. L. "Jonah." In *The Expositor's Bible Commentary.* Vol. 7, *Daniel–Minor Prophets,* edited by Frank E. Gaebelein, 361–91. Grand Rapids: Zondervan, 1985.

Eslinger, Lyle. "Inner-Biblical Exegesis and Inner-Biblical Allusion: The Question of Category." *Vetus Testamentum* 42 (1992) 48–56.

Fiddes, Paul S. "The Canon as Space and Place." In *Einheit der Schrift und die Vielfalt des Kanons = The Unity of Scripture and the Diversity of the Canon,* edited by John Barton and Michael Wolter, 127–49. Beihefte zur Zeitschrift für die neutestamentliche Wissenschaft und die Kunde der älteren Kirche 118. Berlin: de Gruyter, 2003.

Fishbane, Michael. *Biblical Interpretation in Ancient Israel.* Oxford: Clarendon, 1985.

———. "Revelation and Tradition: Aspects of Inner-Biblical Exegesis." *Journal of Biblical Literature* 99 (1980) 343–61.

Floyd, Michael H. "The Chimerical Acrostic of Nahum 1:2–10." *Journal of Biblical Literature* 113 (1994) 421–37.

Franz, Matthias. *Der barmherzige und gnädige Gott: Die Gnadenrede vom Sinai (Exodus 34,6–7) und ihre Parallelen im Alten Testament und seiner Umwelt.* Beiträge zur Wissenschaft vom Alten und Neuen Testament 160. Stuttgart: Kohlhammer, 2003.

Freedman, David Noel. "God Compassionate and Gracious." *Western Watch* 6 (1955) 6–24.

Fretheim, Terrence E. *Exodus.* Interpretation, a Bible Commentary for Teaching and Preaching. Louisville: Westminster John Knox, 1991.

———. *The Message of Jonah: A Theological Commentary.* Minneapolis: Augsburg, 1977. Reprinted, Eugene, OR: Wipf & Stock, 2000.

Garrett, Duane A. *Hosea, Joel*. New American Commentary 19A. Nashville: Broadman & Holman, 1997.

Gerstenberger, Erhard S. *Theologies in the Old Testament*. Translated by John Bowden. Minneapolis: Fortress, 2002.

———. *Wesen und Herkunft des 'apodiktischen Rechts'*. Wissenschaftliche Monographien zum Alten und Neuen Testament 20. 1965. Reprinted, Eugene, OR: Wipf & Stock, 2009.

Glueck, Nelson. *Hesed in the Bible*. Translated by Alfred Gottschalk. Cincinnati: Hebrew Union College Press, 1967.

Good, Edwin M. *Irony in the Old Testament*. Philadelphia: Westminster, 1965.

Graupner, Axel. "Zwei Arbeiten zum Dekalog." *Verkündigung und Forschung* 31 (1986) 308–29.

Gray, George B. *Critical and Exegetical Commentary on Numbers*. International Critical Commentary 4. Edinburgh: T. & T. Clark, 1903.

Gunkel, Hermann. *Introduction to the Psalms: The Genres of the Religious Lyric of Israel*. Completed by Joachim Begrich. Translated by James Nogalski. Mercer Library of Biblical Studies. Macon, GA: Mercer, 1998.

———. "The Close of Micah." In *What Remains of the Old Testament and Other Essays*, translated by A. K. Dallas, 115–50. New York: Macmillan, 1928.

Hagstrom, David G. *The Coherence of the Book of Micah: A Literary Analysis*. SBL Dissertation Series 89. Atlanta: Scholars, 1988.

Haldar, Alfred. *Studies in the Book of Nahum*. Uppsala Universitets Årsskrift 1946:7 Uppsala: Lundeuistska, 1947.

Hamilton, Victor P. "פָּקַד." In *Theological Wordbook of the Old Testament*, edited by R. Laird Harris, et al., 2:731–32. 2 vols. Chicago: Moody, 1980.

Harris, R. Laird, et al., editors. *Theological Wordbook of the Old Testament*. 2 vols. Chicago: Moody, 1980.

Harris, Scott L. *Proverbs 1–9: A Study of Inner-Biblical Interpretation*. SBL Dissertation Series 150. Atlanta: Scholars, 1995.

Haupt, Paul. "The Book of Nahum." *Journal of Biblical Literature* 26 (1907) 1–53.

Holbert, John C. "'Deliverance Belongs to Yahweh!': Satire in the Book of Jonah." In *The Prophets*, edited by Philip R. Davies, 334–54. Biblical Seminar 42. Sheffield, UK: Sheffield Academic, 1996.

Holladay, William Lee. *The Psalms through Three Thousand Years: Prayerbook of a Cloud of Witnesses*. Minneapolis: Fortress, 1993.

Holm-Nielson, Svend. "The Importance of Late Jewish Psalmody for the Understanding of Old Testament Psalmodic Tradition." *Studia Theologica* 14 (1960) 1–53.

Hossfeld, Frank-Lothar, *Der Dekalog: Seine späten Fassungen, die originale Komposition und seine Vorstufen*. Orbis biblicus et orientalis 45. Göttingen: Vandenhoeck & Ruprecht, 1982.

Hossfeld, Frank-Lothar, and Erich Zenger. *Die Psalmen 1: Psalm 1–50*. Neue Echter Bibel. Würzburg: Echter, 1993.

———. *Psalms 2: A Commentary*. Translated by Linda M. Maloney. Hermeneia. Minneapolis: Fortress, 2005.

House, Paul R. "Dramatic Coherence in Nahum, Habakkuk, and Zephaniah." In *Forming Prophetic Literature: Essays on Isaiah and the Twelve in Honor of John D. W. Watts*, edited by James W. Watts and Paul R. House, 195–208. Journal for the Study of the Old Testament Supplement Series 235. Sheffield, UK: Sheffield Academic, 1996.

———. "The Character of God in the Book of the Twelve." In *Reading and Hearing the Book of the Twelve*, edited by James D. Nogalski and Marvin A. Sweeney, 125–45. Society of Biblical Literature Symposium Series 15. Atlanta: Society of Biblical Literature, 2000.

———. *The Unity of the Twelve*. Bible and Literature Series 27. Sheffield, UK: Almond, 1990.

Jacobs, Mignon R. *The Conceptual Coherence of the Book of Micah.* Journal for the Study of the Old Testament Supplement Series 322. Sheffield, UK: Sheffield Academic, 2001.

Janzen, J. Gerald. *Exodus.* Westminster Bible Companion. Louisville: Westminster John Knox, 1997.

Jenni, Ernst, and Claus Westermann, editors. *Theological Lexicon of the Old Testament.* Translated by Mark E. Biddle. Peabody, MA: Hendrickson, 1997.

Jensen, Robert W. *Systematic Theology.* Vol. 1, *The Triune God.* New York: Oxford, 1997.

Jeppesen, Knud. "New Aspects of Micah Research." *Journal for the Study of the Old Testament* 8 (1978) 3–32.

Jepsen, Alfred. "Kleine Beiträge zum Zwölfprophetenbuch." *Zeitschrift für die alttestamentliche Wissenschaft* 56 (1938) 85–100.

———. "Kleine Beiträge zum Zwölfprophetenbuch II." *Zeitschrift für die alttestamentliche Wissenschaft* 57 (1939) 242–55.

Jeremias, Jörg. *Kultprophetie und Gerichtsverküdigung in der späten Königszeit Israels.* Wissenschaftliche Monographien zum Alten und Neuen Testament 35. Neukirchen-Vluyn: Neukirchener, 1970.

Johnstone, William. *Exodus.* Old Testament Guides. Sheffield, UK: JSOT Press, 1990.

———. "The Decalogue and the Redaction of the Sinai Pericope in Exodus." *Zeitschrift für die alttestamentliche Wissenschaft* 100 (1988) 361–85.

———. "The 'Ten Commandments': Some Recent Interpretations." *Expository Times* 100 (1988–1989) 453–61.

Kaiser, Otto, editor. *Texte aus der Umwelt des Alten Testaments.* Gütersloh: Mohn, 1983.

Kapff, Burkhard M. "The Perspective on the Nations in the Book of Micah as a 'Systematization' of the Nations' Role in Joel, Jonah, and Nahum? Reflections on a Context-Oriented Exegesis." In *Thematic Threads in the Book of the Twelve*, edited by Paul L. Redditt and Aaron Schart 292–312. Beihefte zur Zeitschrift für die alttestamentliche Wissenschaft 325. New York: de Gruyter, 2003.

Kidner, Derek. *Ezra and Nehemiah: An Introduction and Commentary.* Tyndale Old Testament Commentaries. Leicester, UK: Inter-Varsity, 1979.

———. *Psalms 73–150: A Commentary on Books III–V of the Psalms.* London: Inter-Varsity, 1975.

Kimelman, Reuven. "Psalm 145: Theme, Structure, and Impact." *Journal of Biblical Literature* 113 (1994) 37–58.

Kittel, Rudolph Wilhelm. et al., editors. *Biblia Hebraica Stuttgartensia.* Stuttgart: Deutsche Bibelstiftung, 1967.

Knight, Douglas. *Rediscovering the Traditions of Israel.* SBL Dissertation Series 9. Missoula: Scholars, 1975.

Knierim Rolf P., and George W. Coats. *Numbers.* Forms of Old Testament Literature 4. Grand Rapids: Eerdmans, 2005.

Kraus, Hans-Joachim. *Psalms 60–150: A Commentary.* Translated by Hilton C. Oswald. Continental Commentaries. Minneapolis: Augsburg Fortress, 1989.

Kristeva, Julia. *Desire in Language: A Semiotic Approach to Literature and Art.* Edited by L. S. Roudiez. Translated by T. Gora, A. Jardine, and L. S. Roudiez. New York: Columbia University Press, 1980.

———. "Word, Dialogue and Novel." In *The Kristeva Reader,* edited by Toril Moi, 34–61. New York: Columbia University Press, 1986.

Kselman, John S. "Psalm 77 and the Book of Exodus." *Journal of the Ancient Near Eastern Society* 15 (1983) 51–58.

Lang, B. "Neues über den Dekalog." *Theologische Quartalschrift* 164 (1984) 58–65.

Lee, Won W. *Punishment and Forgiveness in Israel's Migratory Campaign.* Grand Rapids: Eerdmans, 2003.

Lescow, Theodor. "Redaktionsgeschichtliche Analyse von Micha 1–5." *Zeitschrift für die alttestamentliche Wissenschaft* 84 (1972) 46–85.

———. "Redaktionsgeschichtliche Analyse von Micha 6–7." *Zeitschrift für die alttestamentliche Wissenschaft* 84 (1972) 182–212.

Levin, C. "Der Dekalog am Sinai." *Vetus Testamentum* 35 (1985) 165–91.

Levinson, Bernard M. "Calum M. Carmichael's Approach to the Laws of Deuteronomy." *Harvard Theological Review* 83 (1990) 227–57.

———. *Deuteronomy and the Hermeneutics of Legal Innovation.* New York: Oxford University Press, 1997.

Liebreich, Leon J. "Psalms 34 and 145 in the Light of Their Key Words." *Hebrew Union College Annual* 27 (1956) 181–92.

Lindbeck, George. *The Nature of Doctrine: Religion and Theology in a Postliberal Age.* Louisville: Westminster John Knox, 1984.

Lohfink, Norbert. "The Decalogue of Deuteronomy 5." In *Theology of the Pentateuch: Themes of the Priestly Narrative and Deuteronomy,* translated by Linda M. Maloney, 248–64. Minneapolis: Fortress, 1994.

Luker, L.M. "Doom and Hope in Micah: The Redaction of the Oracles Attributed to an Eighth-Century Prophet." PhD diss., Vanderbilt University, 1985.

Maier, Walter A. *The Book of Nahum: A Commentary.* St. Louis: Concordia, 1959.

Marcus, David. *From Balaam to Jonah: Anti-Prophetic Satire in the Hebrew Bible.* Brown Judaic Studies 301. Atlanta: Scholars, 1995.

Mays, James Luther. *Micah: A Commentary.* Old Testament Library. Philadelphia: Westminster, 1976.

———. *Psalms.* Interpretation. Louisville: John Knox, 1994.

McCann, J. Clinton. *A Theological Introduction to the Book of Psalms: The Psalms as Torah.* Nashville: Abingdon, 1993.

———. "Books I–III and the Editorial Purpose of the Hebrew Psalter." In *The Shape and Shaping of the Psalter,* edited by J. Clinton McCann, 93–107. Journal for the Study of the Old Testament Supplement Series 159. Sheffield, UK: JSOT Press, 1993.

———. "Psalm 73: A Microcosm of Old Testament Theology." In *The Listening Heart: Essays in Wisdom and the Psalms in Honor of Roland E. Murphy,* edited by Kenneth Hoglund 247–57. Journal for the Study of the Old Testament Supplement Series 58. Sheffield, UK: JSOT Press, 1987.

———. "Psalms." In *1 & 2 Maccabees, Job, Psalms,* edited by Leander Keck, 641–1280. New Interpreter's Bible 4. Nashville: Abingdon, 1996.

McCarthy, Dennis. *Treaty and Covenant: A Study in Form in the Ancient Oriental Documents and in the Old Testament.* 2nd ed. Analecta Biblica 21A. Rome: Biblical Institute Press, 1981.

McEvenue, Sean. "A Source Critical Problem in Num.14,26–38." *Biblica* 50 (1969) 454–56.

Mendenhall, George E. "Ancient Oriental and Biblical Law." *Biblical Archaeologist* 27 (1954) 26–46.

———. "Covenant Forms in Israelite Tradition." *Biblical Archaeologist* 27 (1954) 50–76.

Merx, Adalbert. *Die Prophetie des Joel und ihre Ausleger von den ältesten Zeiten bis zu den Reformatoren.* Halle: Verlag der Buchhandlung des Waisenhauses, 1879.

Mettinger, Tryggve N. D. "The Veto on Images and the Aniconic God in Ancient Israel." In *Religious Symbols and Their Functions*, 15–29. Scripta Instituti Donneriani Aboensis 10. Stockholm: Almqvist & Wiksell, 1979.

Michel-Mainz, Andreas. "Ist mit der 'Gnadenformel' von Ex 34,6(+7?) der Schlüssel zu einer Theologie des Alten Testaments gefunden?" *Biblische Notizen* 118 (2003) 110–23.

Milgrom, Jacob. *Numbers* = במדבר: *The Traditional Hebrew Text with the New JPS Translation Commentary.* The JPS Torah Commentary. Philadelphia: Jewish Publication Society, 1990.

Moberly, R. W. L. *At the Mountain of God: Story and Theology in Exodus 32–34.* Journal for the Study of the Old Testament Supplement Series 22. Sheffield, UK: JSOT Press, 1983.

Mowinckel, Sigmund. *Le Décalogue.* Études d'histoire et de philosophie religieuses 16 Paris: Alcan, 1927.

———. *Psalms in Israel's Worship.* Translated by D. R. Ap-Thomas. 2 vols. Oxford: Blackwell, 1962.

Nicholson, Ernest W. *Deuteronomy and Tradition.* Philadelphia: Fortress, 1967.

Nelson, Richard D. *Deuteronomy: A Commentary.* Old Testament Library. Louisville: Westminster John Knox, 2002.

Newing, Edward G. "The Rhetoric of Altercation in Numbers 14." In *Perspectives on Language and Text: Essays and Poems in Honor of Francis I. Andersen's Sixtieth Birthday*, edited by Edgar W. Conrad and Edward G. Newing, 211–28. Winona Lake, IN: Eisenbrauns, 1987.

Nielson, Eduard. *Ten Commandments in New Perspective: A Traditio-Historical Approach.* Translated by David J. Bourke. Studies in Biblical Theology, 2nd ser. 7. Naperville: IL: Allenson, 1968.

Nogalski, James D. "Joel as a 'Literary Anchor' for the Book of the Twelve." In *Reading and Hearing the Book of the Twelve*, edited by James D. Nogalski and Marvin A. Sweeney, 91–109. SBL Symposium Series 15. Atlanta: Society of Biblical Literature, 2000.

———. *Literary Precursors to the Book of the Twelve.* Beihefte zur Zeitschrift für die alttestamentliche Wissenschaft 217. New York: de Gruyter, 1993.

———. *Redactional Processes in the Book of the Twelve.* Beihefte zur Zeitschrift für die alttestamentliche Wissenschaft 218. Berlin: de Gruyter, 1993.

———. "The Redactional Shaping of Nahum 1 for the Book of the Twelve." In *Among the Prophets: Language, Image and Structure in the Prophetic Writings*, edited by Philip R. Davies and David J. A. Clines, 193–202. Journal for the Study of the Old Testament Supplement Series 144. Sheffield, UK: JSOT Press, 1993.

———. "The Use of Stichwörter as a Redactional Unification Technique in the Book of the Twelve." ThM thesis, Baptist Theological Seminary, Ruschlikon, Switzerland, 1987.

Nogalski, James D., and Marvin A. Sweeney, editors. *Reading and Hearing the Book of the Twelve.* SBL Symposium Series 15. Atlanta: Society of Biblical Literature, 2000.

Noth, Martin. *Numbers: A Commentary.* Old Testament Library. Translated by James D. Martin. Philadelphia: Westminster, 1963.

Obbink, H. T. "Jahwebilder." *Zeitschrift für die alttestamentliche Wissenschaft* 46 (1929) 264–74.

O'Brien, Julia M. *Nahum.* Readings, A New Biblical Commentary. London: Sheffield, UK: Academic, 2002.

Odel, Margaret S. "The Prophets and the End of Hosea." In *Forming Prophetic Literature: Essays on Isaiah and the Twelve in Honor of John D. W. Watts,* edited by James W. Watts and Paul R. House 160–69. Journal for the Study of the Old Testament Supplement Series 235. Sheffield, UK: Sheffield Academic, 1996.

Oesterley, William O. E. *The Psalms: Translated with Text-Critical and Exegetical Notes.* London: SPCK, 1962.

Ogden, Graham S., and Richard R. Deutsch. *A Promise of Hope—A Call to Obedience: A Commentary of the Books of Joel and Malachi.* International Theological Commentary. Grand Rapids: Eerdmans, 1987.

Olson, Dennis T. *Numbers.* Interpretation. Louisville: John Knox, 1996.

Parker, N. H. "Psalm 103: God is Love. He Will Have Mercy and Abundantly Pardon." *Canadian Journal of Theology* 1 (1955) 191–96.

Perdue, Leo G. *Wisdom and Cult: A Critical Analysis of the Views of Cult in the Wisdom Literature of Israel and the Ancient Near East.* SBL Dissertation Series 30. Missoula, MT: Scholars, 1977.

Perlitt, Lothar. *Bundestheologie im Alten Testament.* Wissenschaftliche Monographien zum Alten und Neuen Testament 36. Neukirchen-Vluyn: Neukirchener, 1969.

Perry, Menakhem. "Literary Dynamics: How the Order of a Text Creates its Meaning." *Poetics Today* 1 (1975) 35–64, 311–61.

Person, Raymond F., Jr. *In Conversation with Jonah: Conversation Analysis, Literary Criticism, and the Book of Jonah.* Journal for the Study of the Old Testament Supplement Series 220. Sheffield, UK: Sheffield Academic, 1996.

Peterson, David L. "A Book of the Twelve?" In *Reading and Hearing the Book of the Twelve,* edited by James D. Nogalski and Marvin A. Sweeney 3–10. Society of Biblical Literature Symposium Series 15. Atlanta: Society of Biblical Literature, 2000.

Pigott, Susan. "God of Compassion and Mercy: An Analysis of the Background, Use and Theological Significance of Exodus 34:6–7." PhD diss., Southwestern Baptist Theological Seminary, 1995.

Pope, Marvin. *El in the Ugaritic Texts.* Supplements to Vetus Testamentum 2. Leiden: Brill, 1955.

Pritchard, James B., editor. *Ancient Near Eastern Texts: Relating to the Old Testament.* 3rd ed. Princeton: Princeton University Press, 1969.

Rabinowitz, Peter. "End Sinister: Neat Closure as Disruptive Force." In *Reading Narrative: Form, Ethics, Ideology,* edited by James Phelan, 120–31. Columbus: Ohio State University Press, 1989.

Rad, Gerhard von. "The Form-Critical Problem of the Hexateuch." In *The Problem of the Hexateuch and Other Essays,* translated by E. W. Trueman Dicken, 1–78. New York: McGraw-Hill, 1966.

———. *Old Testament Theology.* 2 vols. Translated by D. M. G. Stalker. New York: Harper & Row, 1962–1965.

———. *The Problem of the Hexateuch and Other Essays.* Translated by E. W. Trueman Dicken. New York: McGraw-Hill, 1966.

Raitt, Thomas. "Why Does God Forgive?" *Horizons in Biblical Theology* 13 (1991) 38–58.

Redditt, Paul L. "The Book of Joel and Peripheral Prophecy." *Catholic Biblical Quarterly* 48 (1986) 225–40.

———. "Recent Research on the Book of the Twelve as One Book." *Currents in Research: Biblical Studies* 9 (2001) 47–80.

Redditt, Paul L., and Aaron Schart, editors. *Thematic Threads in the Book of the Twelve*. Beihefte zur Zeitschrift für die alttestamentliche Wissenschaft 325. New York: de Gruyter, 2003.

Reventlow, Henning G. *Gebot und Predigt im Dekalog*. Gütersloh: Mohn, 1962.

Roberts, J. J. M. *Nahum, Habakkuk and Zephaniah*. Old Testament Library. Louisville: Westminster John Knox, 1991.

Sakenfield, Katherine Doob. *Journeying with God: A Commentary on the Book of Numbers*. International Theological Commentary. Grand Rapids: Eerdmans, 1995.

———. *The Meaning of* Hesed *in the Hebrew Bible: A New Enquiry*. Harvard Semitic Monographs 17. Missoula, MT: Scholars, 1978.

Sanders, J. A. *Canon and Community: A Guide to Canonical Criticism*. Guides to Biblical Scholarship. Philadelphia: Fortress, 1984.

———. *The Dead Sea Psalms Scroll*. Ithaca: Cornell University Press, 1967.

Sarna, Nahum M. *Exodus =[Shemot]: The Traditional Hebrew Text with the New JPS Commentary*. Philadelphia: Jewish Publication Society, 1991.

———. "Psalm 89: A Study in Inner Biblical Exegesis." In *Biblical and Other Studies*, edited by Alexander Altmann, 29–46. Studies and Texts 1. Cambridge: Harvard University Press, 1963.

Scharbert, Josef. "Formgeschichte und Exegese Von Ex 34,6f und Seiner Parallelen." *Biblica* 38 (1957) 130–50.

Schart, Aaron. *Die Entstehung des Zwölfprophetenbuchs: Neubearbeitungen von Amos im Rahmen schriftenübergreifender Redaktionsprozesse*. Beihefte zur Zeitschrift für die alttestamentliche Wissenschaft 260. Berlin: de Gruyter, 1998.

Schmidt, Ludwig. "Die Kundschaftererzählung in Num 13–14 und Dtn 1,19–46: Eine Kritik neurer Pentateuchkritik." *Zeitschrift für die alttestamentliche Wissenschaft* 114 (2002) 40–58.

Schmidt, Werner H. *Königtum Gottes in Ugarit und Israel: Zur Herkunft der Königsprädikation Jahwes*. 2nd ed. Beihefte zur Zeitschrift für die alttestamentliche Wissenschaft 80 Berlin: Töpelmann, 1966.

Schultz, Hermann. *Das Buch Nahum: Eine redaktionskritische Untersuchung*. Beihefte zur Zeitschrift für die alttestamentliche Wissenchaft 129. Berlin: de Gruyter, 1973.

Scoralick, Ruth. *Gottes Güte und Gottes Zorn: Die Gottesprädikationen in Exodus 34,6f und Ihre Intertextuellen Beziehungen Zum Zwölfprophetenbuch*. Herders Biblische Studien 33. Freiburg: Herder, 2002.

Shaw, Charles S. *The Speeches of Micah: A Rhetorical-Historical Analysis*. Journal for the Study of the Old Testament Supplement Series 145. Sheffield, UK: JSOT Press, 1993.

Simundson, Daniel J. *Hosea, Joel, Amos, Obadiah, Jonah, Micah*. Abingdon Old Testament Commentaries. Nashville: Abingdon, 2005.

Smart, James D. "The Book of Jonah: Introduction and Exegesis." In *The Interpreter's Bible*. Vol. 6, *Lamentations, Ezekiel, Daniel, and the Book of the Twelve*, edited by George A. Buttrick, 871–94. New York: Abingdon, 1956.

Smith, Billy O. "The Reconciliation of the Moral Attributes of Yahweh as Revealed in Exodus 34:6–7." ThD diss., New Orleans Baptist Theological Seminary, 1953.

Smith, George A. *The Book of the Twelve Prophets*. Expositor's Bible. New York: Armstrong, 1903.

Smith, Ralph L. *Micah–Malachi*. Word Biblical Commentary 32. Waco, TX: Word, 1984.

———. *Old Testament Theology: Its History, Method, and Message*. Nashville: Broadman & Holman, 1993.

Spieckermann, Hermann. "'Barmherzig und gnädig ist der Herr . . .'" *Zeitschrift für die alttestamentliche Wissenschaft* 102 (1990) 1–18.

Spronk, Klaas. *Nahum*. Historical Commentary on the Old Testament. Kampen, Netherlands: Pharos, 1997.

Stamm, Johann J. and M. E. Andrew, *The Ten Commandments in Recent Research*. Studies in Biblical Theology 2nd ser., 2. Naperville, IL: Allenson, 1967.

Stansell, Gary. *Micah and Isaiah: A Form and Tradition Historical Comparison*. SBL Dissertation Series 85. Atlanta: Scholars, 1988.

Tate, Marvin E. *Psalms 51–100*. Word Biblical Commentary 20. Waco, TX: Word, 1990.

Thompson, John A. "The Book of Joel." In *The Interpreter's Bible*. Vol. 6, *Lamentations, Ezekiel, Daniel and the Book of the Twelve*, edited by George A. Buttrick, 729–60. New York: Abingdon, 1956.

Thordarson, Thorir K. "The Form-Historical Problem of Ex. 34:6–7." PhD diss., University of Chicago Divinity School, 1959.

Trible, Phyllis. *God and the Rhetoric of Sexuality*. Overtures to Biblical Theology. Philadelphia: Fortress, 1978.

Upensky, Boris. *A Poetics of Composition: The Structure of the Artistic Text and Typology of a Compositional Form*. Translated by Calentina Zavarin and Susan Wittig. Berkeley: University of California Press, 1973.

Van Gemeren, Willem, editor. *New International Dictionary of Old Testament Theology & Exegesis*. 5 vols. Grand Rapids: Zondervan, 1996.

Van Leeuwen, Raymond. "Scribal Wisdom and Theodicy in the Book of the Twelve." In *In Search of Wisdom: Essays in Memory of John Gammie*, edited by Leo Perdue, et al., 31–49. Louisville: Westminster John Knox, 1993.

Van Seters, John. *A Law Book for the Diaspora: Revision in the Study of the Covenant Code*. Oxford: Oxford University Press, 2003.

———. "The Pentateuch." In *The Hebrew Bible Today: An Introduction to Critical Issues*, edited by Steven L. McKenzie and M. Patrick Graham, 1–49. Louisville: Westminster John Knox, 1998.

Walton, John H. "Deuteronomy: An Exposition of the Spirit of the Law." *Grace Theological Journal* 8 (1987) 213–25.

———. "Psalms: A Cantata about the Davidic Covenant." *Journal of the Evangelical Theological Society* 34 (1991) 21–31.

Washington, Harold. "The Lord's Mercy Endures Forever: Toward a Post-Shoah Reading of Grace in the Hebrew Scriptures." *Interpretation* 54 (2000) 135–45.

Watson, Wilfred G. E. "Reversed Rootplay in Ps 145." *Biblica* 62 (1981) 101–102.

Watts, John D. W. "A Frame for the Book of the Twelve: Hosea 1–3 and Malachi." In *Reading and Hearing the Book of the Twelve*, edited by James D. Nogalski and Marvin A. Sweeney, 209–17. SBL Symposium Series 15. Atlanta: Society of Biblical Literature, 2000.

Weinfeld, Moshe. *Deuteronomy 1–11: A New Translation and Commentary*. Anchor Bible 5. New York: Doubleday, 1991.

Weiser, Artur. *The Psalms: A Commentary*. Translated by Herbert Hartwell. Old Testament Library. Philadelphia: Westminster, 1962.

Wellhausen, Julius. *Die Composition des Hexateuchs und der historischen Bücher des Alten Testaments.* Berlin: Reimer, 1989.

Westermann, Claus. *Elements of Old Testament Theology.* Translated by D. W. Stott. Atlanta: John Knox, 1982.

———. *Praise and Lament in the Psalms.* Translated by Keith R. Crim and Richard N. Soulen. Atlanta: John Knox, 1981.

———. *The Living Psalms.* Translated by J. R. Porter. Edinburgh: T. & T. Clark, 1989.

Whybray, Norman. *Reading the Psalms as a Book.* Journal for the Study of the Old Testament Supplement Series 222. Sheffield, UK: Sheffield Academic, 1996.

Whybray, R. N. *The Making of the Pentateuch: A Methodological Study.* Journal for the Study of the Old Testament Supplement Series 53. Sheffield, UK: JSOT Press, 1987.

Williamson, H. G. M. *Ezra, Nehemiah.* Word Biblical Commentary 16. Waco, TX: Word, 1985.

Willis, John T. "Fundamental Issues in Contemporary Micah Studies." *Restoration Quarterly* 13 (1970) 77–90.

———. "Structure of Micah 3–5 and the Function of Micah 5:9–14 in the Book." *Zeitschrift für die alttesamentliche Wissenschaft* 81 (1969) 191–214.

Willis, Timothy M. "'So Great is His Steadfast Love': A Rhetorical Analysis of Psalm 103." *Biblica* 72 (1991) 525–37.

Wilson, Gerald H. "A First Century CE Date for the Closing for the Book of Psalms." *Jewish Bible Quarterly* 28 (2000) 102–10.

———. "Shaping the Psalter: A Consideration of Editorial Linkage in the Book of Psalms." In *The Shape and Shaping of the Psalter,* edited by J. Clinton McCann, 72–82. Journal for the Study of the Old Testament Supplement Series 159. Sheffield: JSOT Press, 1993.

———. *The Editing of the Hebrew Psalter.* SBL Dissertation Series 76; Chico, CA: Scholars, 1985.

———. "The Shape of the Book of Psalms." *Interpretation* 46 (1992) 129–42.

———. "The Use of Royal Psalms at the 'Seams' of the Hebrew Psalter." *Journal for the Study of the Old Testament* 35 (1986) 85–94.

Wolff, Hans Walter. *Micah: A Commentary.* Translated by Gary Stansell. Continental Commentaries. Minneapolis: Augsburg, 1990.

———. *Joel and Amos.* Translated by Waldemar Janzen, et al. Hermenia. Philadelphia: Fortress, 1977.

———. *Studien zum Jonabuch.* Biblische Studien 47. Neukirchen-Vluyn: Neukirchener, 1965.

Wright, G. Ernest. *God Who Acts: Biblical Theology as Recital.* Studies in Biblical Theology 8. London: SCM, 1952.

Young, Edward J. *An Introduction to the Old Testament.* Rev. ed. Grand Rapids: Eerdmans, 1960.

Zobel, "חסד *Hesed.*" In *Theological Dictionary of the Old Testament,* translated by David E. Green, 5:62–64. Grand Rapids: Eerdmans, 1974.

Zimmerli, Walter. "Das zweite Gebot." In *Gottes Offenbarung: gesammelte Aufsätze zum Alten Testament,* 234–48. Theologische Bücherei; Neudrucke und Berichte aus dem 20. Jahrhundert 19. Munich: Kaiser, 1963.

Index of Ancient Documents